T0345302

Can It!

Can It!

The Perils and Pleasures
of Preserving Foods

Gary Allen

For Karen, my enabler-in-chief

Published by Reaktion Books Ltd
Unit 32, Waterside
44–48 Wharf Road
London N1 7UX, UK
www.reaktionbooks.co.uk

First published 2016

Copyright © Gary Allen 2016

All rights reserved
No part of this publication may be reproduced, stored in a
retrieval system, or transmitted, in any form or by any means,
electronic, mechanical, photocopying, recording or otherwise,
without the prior permission of the publishers

Printed and bound in China by 1010 Printing International Ltd

A catalogue record for this book is available from the
British Library

ISBN 978 1 78023 572 1

Contents

Introduction

Humans are not the only species that saves food for leaner times. Some animals simply build up their fat reserves. Some hide their surplus food in places where they can access them later. Only a small number of species alter their food in some way to prevent spoilage. Bees, the prime example, partially dehydrate the nectar of flowers, then preserve it by sealing it in wax. However, though we may not be the only food-preserving species, we certainly preserve more food, in more diverse ways, than any other.

We have always faced the alternating problems of food scarcity and seasonal over-abundance. Our hunter-gatherer forebears tracked their foods, collecting whatever was available in the lands they moved through before travelling on to the next location. They collected wild grass seeds (the ancestors of our corn, wheat, barley and rice), or annual runs of shad or salmon, or a huge variety of fruits, berries and roots. Everything they ate was in season and locally grown. Most was consumed on the spot because – other than easily dried grains and legumes – their foods were perishable. Even if they had storable food, carrying it on their nomadic forays was inconvenient. Later, when agriculture and the domestication of food plants and animals made surpluses possible, food storage for civilizations – large groups of people living together in something like cities – became a necessity. This biblical story recalls the early days of agricultural dependence:

Small jars with jams for tasting at a market.

7

Pharaoh dreamed: and, behold, he stood by the river.

And, behold, there came up out of the river seven well-favoured kine and fat-fleshed; and they fed in a meadow.

And, behold, seven other kine came up after them out of the river, ill favoured and lean-fleshed; and stood by the other kine upon the brink of the river.

And the ill-favoured and lean-fleshed kine did eat up the seven well-favoured and fat kine. So Pharaoh awoke (Genesis 41:1–7).

Fortunately, Joseph interpreted Pharoah's dreams, and established storage facilities for reserving the agricultural output of the good years so that, when the inevitable famine came, 'in all the land of Egypt there was bread.' Pharoah's sufficiently stocked storehouses even permitted exports to less prudent nations. Such long-term food storage required the development of food preservation techniques, and these techniques helped the ancients to achieve what we are still trying to do today: conquer time. We slow or stop the processes that cause decay and loss, and we have discovered how to surmount long distances, allowing perishable foods to travel further than would otherwise be possible. While Moses – or whoever wrote the biblical passage – never specified the techniques used, we know that the ancient Babylonians and Egyptians were already using salt to dry and save foods. Joseph's story is, in essence, a parable about the necessity of food preservation in the ancient world.

Today, many of us eschew food that is neither fresh nor local. We imagine that such foods have diminished nutrition and taste, and waste energy in processing and transportation. In some cases, these suspicions are justified, but not always. As Mark Bittman asks:

I've long wondered how producing a decent ingredient, one that you can buy in any supermarket, really happens. Take canned tomatoes, of which I probably use 100 pounds a year. It costs $2 to $3 a pound to buy hard,

Display of home-
preserved food.

tasteless, 'fresh' plum tomatoes, but only half that for almost two pounds of canned tomatoes that taste much better. How is that possible?[1]

Part of the answer is that the canned tomatoes were picked at the optimum moment of ripeness, not harvested under-ripe to mini-mize damage in handling. They were processed within hours,

WASTE NOT–WANT NOT

PREPARE FOR WINTER

Save Perishable Foods by Preserving Now

instead of the days required by most farmers' markets. Being tinned (canned), they could be shipped in huge, efficient vehicles that did not require the delicate handling of fresh tomatoes. Unless you expertly grow tomatoes yourself, and harvest them at the moment when they are at their best, the canned variety is likely to taste better than any you could preserve for yourself.

Modern preservation processes involve refrigeration, freezing and freeze-drying, radiation, pasteurization, chemical preservatives, vacuum-packing and a host of other methods never imagined by our ancestors. These technologies aim to preserve the nutrition and – as closely as possible – the original flavours and textures of the foods being stored to maintain (or at least mimic) the qualities of fresh foods. Modern technologies also make it possible to produce foodstuffs that travel well and last indefinitely, thus reducing waste and increasing profits. These artificially fresh foods were impossible with only the methods of the past.

Early attempts to pit the problem of seasonal abundance against seasonal scarcity led to the development of ingenious methods, often based on techniques that involved drying, smoking and salting – sometimes alone, sometimes in combination. The cleverest technique was the intentional use of fermentation, which is a form of desirable decay. Our ancestors did not understand chemistry, physics or biology, but their methods did more than save perishable foods; they created a multitude of new foods. The preservation process fundamentally altered the foods, creating new and different flavours and textures. Only a fool would describe wine as elderly grape juice. Cheese – 'milk's leap toward immortality', as Clifton Fadiman quipped – is nothing like modern canned or dehydrated milk. Turning cabbage into sauerkraut or kimchi preserved the vegetable, but also created new flavours and textures. The ancient Romans converted fish scraps and offal into *liquamen*, just as Southeast Asians make *nuóc mâm* or Italians ferment *colatura* today. Chinese hot and sour soup gets its tang in part from vinegar, but also from 'golden needles', the buds of a type of daylily. These

Canada Food Board, poster recommending home preservation, 1914–18.

buds have very little taste when fresh; their distinctive flavour is only developed through bacterial fermentation as they dry. One particular flavour, umami (the so-called 'fifth taste'), is often enhanced or created by fermentation. When certain amino acids are broken into their component glutamates, this savoury new taste emerges. It is one of the distinguishing characteristics of preserved foods from around the world.

The preservation of foods, a process born out of need, but which often transforms the food into something else, has transformed the diets of people around the world, sometimes unifying, but more often contributing to the diversity of the globe's cuisines. When we look closely at our preserved foods, we see our cultural fingerprints all over them. This is not the bad thing Julia Child was bemoaning with her remark about fancy restaurant food ('It's so beautifully arranged on the plate – you know someone's fingers have been all over it'), but more like what Rachel Laudan meant when she said 'we hinder our understanding of food if we don't understand that all our food, with the exception of a few fruits, has been transformed, that is, processed, before we eat it.'[2]

Ancient processes did not just preserve the nutrients of the original foodstuffs, but created flavours that are inseparable from, and may even be said to define, the cuisines and cultures of the cooks who have been making them for centuries. It is, perhaps, not a coincidence that we use the word 'culture' not only for the characteristics that distinguish one social group from another, but for how they modify their foods.

A Couple of Brief Notes

To address the issue of 'processing' versus 'preserving', unless we are picking fruit right off the tree and eating it, we are probably processing it in some way – cooking, peeling, even washing, are all forms of processing. For our purposes, in this book, 'processing' refers to those activities we do in order to make food last longer than its unprocessed version. Often that means the raw food is changed into something quite different from what it was when it was harvested.

There are many quotations from historic sources in this book. Ancient cookbooks and some modern ones can tell us a great deal about safe food preservation; a grain – or perhaps more – of salt may preserve us from some unpleasant gastric experiences. Rather than litter these quotations with 'sics' whenever they include spellings or grammar that fail to suit our modern tastes, they have been left as they were originally written. We prefer to think of them not as mistakes (which they were not, at the time), but as charmingly old-fashioned details. These antique recipes have not been edited to comply with modern methods of preservation or sanitation – or even, in some cases, common sense. Left intact, they can tell us a lot about how our ancestors 'put food by'. They may also leave us wondering how anyone survived long enough to actually write those cookbooks. If you are the sort of person who touches paint to see if it is really wet or tastes unfamiliar mushrooms to see if they are really poisonous, feel free to try some of these unusual recipes – at your own risk.

Just remember: you've been warned.

ONE

Perils

How, in this best of all possible worlds, can there even be such a thing as food spoilage? One not-so-serious answer is that we have been booted out of the Garden of Eden, and we get what we deserve. The real reason is that all sorts of living things want our food, just as we do, because food contains the nutrients and stored energy that living things need to survive.

Normally, we wouldn't mind sharing with 'wee sleekit beasties' – providing they do not take more than their share. Unfortunately, once they discover a rich supply of nutrients, they multiply like crazy and literally eat us out of house and home. One of the reasons our ancestors domesticated cats, which provide neither food, milk, fur nor muscle power, is that they were very good at reducing the rodent populations in early granaries.

Theft is not the most troublesome aspect of infestations. Whatever is ingested must also be excreted. In many (but, as we will see, not all) cases, it is the waste products from all that consumption that bothers us most. Droppings and urine are foul smelling, and therefore not something we want in our food. Presumably, they are foul tasting as well, but not many food connoisseurs are likely to volunteer to confirm this hypothesis. Worse, these waste products contain vast quantities of bacteria. Bacteria also love the nutrients in our foods, and likewise produce large quantities of waste – waste that can render our food unpalatable or make us ill. Not only that, but the moisture in rodent urine can make even

One-pint 'Quick Seal' glass-topped jar, with wire bail, for home preserving; made between 1910 and 1930.

dry grain susceptible to moulds, yeasts and fungi – and yes, these microorganisms also produce toxins that make our lives miserable. To add insult to injury, the odours created by all this biological activity attract insects, which are eager to join in the feast, and bring along even more unpleasant microorganisms.

Food spoilage is a nasty process that accelerates as the various carriers increase exponentially. It only stops when there is nothing left to consume. We have not always known how this spoilage occurred but we learned, early on, that the best way to avoid it was to prevent it from starting. Cats are fur-bearing, food-preserving devices, and early allies in our war against decay.

While animals can carry the organisms that lead to spoilage, they are not the only delivery system. Pathogens can arrive in water. Many of them, like bacteria and the spores of yeasts and moulds, are tiny enough to be carried by the wind. Even if we could ensure that the water was sterile, and the air filtered of all contaminants, our food would still spoil. It contains the seeds of its own destruction.

Grain, once the seeds of wild grasses, became the earliest domesticated crop. It's an ideal food for storing; as long as it's kept dry and free of rats and mice, it will last practically forever.

Millions of microorganisms inhabit every living thing, many of which are essential to its normal functions. Our guts (and those of all animals, including the ones we eat) contain bacteria that aid the digestion of food. Some break complex molecules into smaller, more accessible ones; some secrete digestive enzymes that our bodies cannot produce. It is a symbiotic relationship whereby the bacteria get the nutrients and energy that they need while freeing up an excess of these substances for our use.

So, why don't these beneficial bacteria get greedy and eat us? They would, except that our bodies evolved alongside the bacteria, and have developed control systems that establish a kind of détente that is beneficial to both parties. When an animal dies, and those control systems cease to function, microorganisms finally get the upper hand and the spoilage begins – even if no outside sources of contamination are present.

Several factors affect the speed of spoilage: is the environment warm enough, but not too warm? Is there enough water to support a growing colony of pathogens? Is the chemical environment conducive to growth? If the answer to these questions is 'yes', the spoilers multiply rapidly. If the temperature is too high, the bacteria or other unwanted organisms are killed. If it is too low, the organisms' rate of reproduction slows to a virtual standstill. If there is insufficient moisture, the reproduction rate slows or even stops. Certain chemicals discourage growth or even kill the organisms that cause spoilage, and they do so by a number of different methods.

Before deciding on the right tactic for preventing food spoilage, we should identify some of the main culprits. Most are bacteria – the tiny unseen beings we tend to lump together as 'germs' – but some other forms of minuscule miscreants also get to us through our food. One of the major players is *Salmonella*, a genus of over 2,000 species (two of them, *S. enteritidis* and *S. typhimurium*, are responsible for the majority of our cases of food poisoning). The bacteria live in the intestines of animals, and are spread by faecal contamination. Meat (muscle tissue) generally becomes exposed to the bacteria during slaughter, although foods can be cross-contaminated when undercooked juices come into contact with pre-cooked foods, or foods that might otherwise be safely eaten raw.

The symptoms of salmonellosis – chills, headache, nausea and vomiting – may appear at any time from eight hours to three days after contaminated eggs, meat, milk and dairy products, poultry or seafood are eaten, and can continue for up to a week. The disease affects over one million people a year in the U.S., causing some 400 deaths. Most cases of salmonellosis are caused by contaminated fresh foods; however, nine people died between 2008 and 2009 when 700 people were sickened by peanut butter. The frozen Nakaochi scrape (small bits of fish scraped off the bones after the fish has been filleted) of yellowfin tuna, used in spicy tuna sushi, poisoned 425 people in 2012. The largest-scale contamination affected 36 million pounds of frozen ground turkey in 2011 in the U.S.; because it was recognized early, and the meat was removed from supermarkets, only one person died.

Eggs become infected with *Salmonella* inside the chicken, before a protective shell has formed. No amount of care between hen and table, other than cooking to temperatures high enough to produce overcooked eggs, can protect us from that form of food poisoning. There is one method of prevention:

> Since the late 1990s, British farmers have been vaccinating hens against salmonella . . . this measure has virtually wiped out the health threat in Britain. In 1997, there were 14,771 reported cases of salmonella poisoning there, by 2009 this had dropped to just 581 cases. About 90 per cent of British eggs now come from vaccinated hens.[1]

Think of it as food preservation through prevention. While the bacteria of *Salmonella* are a leading cause of food-borne illness in the U.S., they can be rendered harmless by thorough cooking, or by scrupulous attention to sanitation at all stages of processing.

Campylobacter jejuni is the second-most frequent cause of food poisoning in the U.S. Like *Salmonella*, it lives in the digestive systems of species that we like to eat: cattle, pigs, domesticated poultry and game birds. Again, as with *Salmonella*, we can acquire it through consumption of unpasteurized milk, raw or under-cooked meat or poultry, or other contaminated foods. Some people are unaffected by *Campylobacter*, while others can develop symptoms of campylobacteriosis after consuming as few as 500 cells. It incubates in between two and ten days, and symptoms can last for a week. The disease can cause abdominal cramps, bloody diarrhoea and fever. In rare cases, the disease can progress to meningitis or even Guillain-Barré syndrome. Over 100 people die each year from *Campylobacter*-caused illnesses, which could be prevented through the same methods used to prevent salmonellosis. Unlike in the UK,

> In contrast, there is no such requirement for commercial hens in the U.S. Consequently, according to FDA data, there are about 142,000 illnesses every year caused by consuming eggs contaminated by the most common strain of salmonella. Only about one-third of farmers here choose to inoculate their flocks.[2]

Listeria monocytogenes is a species of bacteria that occurs naturally in soil and water. It is easily taken up by farm animals, especially cows and chickens, that then pass it along, both to their products and to the facilities that process them. *Listeria* are easily killed by cooking. However, if the properly cooked and chilled foods are reinfected by cross-contamination, new infestations can thrive even in cold refrigerators.

Consuming infected raw milk products (such as unpasteurized Brie, Camembert, feta or queso fresco) or processed meats (such as cold cuts, hot dogs, pâtés and spreadable potted meats) can cause listeriosis. The disease appears between three and 70 days after consuming contaminated food, and can last for weeks. It sometimes begins with diarrhoea, followed by confusion, fever, stiff neck, vomiting and weakness. In 2002, 30 million pounds of American pre-sliced turkey had to be destroyed after listeriosis sickened 46 people and killed eight others.

Staphylococcus aureus, a bacterium that lives on the skin of people and animals, can multiply under ideal conditions and produce virulent toxins that cause staphyloenterotoxicosis. The symptoms (diarrhoea, stomach cramps, nausea and vomiting) begin from 30 minutes to six hours after consuming contaminated food. Contamination can be easily prevented by good sanitation. *Staphylococci* can be killed by heat, but cooking does not destroy the toxins they produce. Consequently, it is critical to avoid cross-contaminating cooked food by preventing contact with uncooked food or with hands (or surfaces) that might have been exposed to the uncooked food.

Bacillus cereus, various *Vibrio* species and *Yersinia enterocolitica* are often involved with cases of less serious food poisoning, but they are not generally associated with preserved foods (although *B. cereus* can survive for long periods under refrigeration).

Yeasts are single-celled fungi that account for plenty of food spoilage, as well as some food poisoning. Some species of *Aspergillus*, *Claviceps*, *Fusarium* and *Penicillium* are the primary genera of concern. All fungi require moisture, so it is essential that the foods upon which fungi might feed be kept dry.

We have another reason to be concerned about fungal contamination of food. While low temperatures significantly slow bacterial growth, fungi are not so easily discouraged. They can thrive at a chilly 0°C (32°F). Not only that, acidic foods (like salsa or yoghurt) that inhibit the spread of bacteria can provide a happy home for mould. If you have ever opened a long-forgotten jar at the back of a refrigerator shelf, you will probably recall – with a brief, involuntary shudder – a furry encounter with mould. Even very dry foods, like stale bread, can produce colonies of mould. Sugary or salty foods – jam and ham, for example – which are immune to colonization by bacteria, are hospitable to fungi. In fact, once bacteria are no longer in competition for the nutrients in our foods, moulds and yeasts have an easier time of it.

Yeasts can produce a number of mycotoxins, the aflatoxins produced by *A. flavius* and *A. parasiticus* being most significant. Aflatoxins can trigger a range of ill effects: from liver damage, abdominal pain and convulsions, to the disruption of digestion, absorption or metabolism of food, oedema, haemorrhage, mental impairment, vomiting, comatose states and even death. Other mycotoxins cause cancers of the organs (heart, liver, kidney) or nerves, gastrointestinal distress, immune system dysfunction and reproductive problems.

Mycotoxins are most commonly found in cereal grains, coffee, dairy products, fruits, nuts and spices. The most famous examples are the ergot alkaloids found in badly stored rye. Confirmed out-breaks of ergotism, caused by *Claviceps purpurea*, date to 857 CE, but even as recently as 2006, 125 Kenyans died after they ate corn contaminated with aflatoxins. Mycotoxins in animal feed can pass through eggs, meat and milk to affect humans.

Airborne and waterborne fungal spores are everywhere, but the biggest source is the food itself. It has been exposed to the air, possibly in many locations, before arriving in our kitchens. Even if we have been successful in preventing spores from coming in, the food can be contaminated by improperly cleaned equipment, or by the packaging that holds our finished products.

Food-based illnesses can also result from viruses (Noro-virus and Rotavirus), protozoa (*Cryptosporidium*, *Entamoeba* and *Giardia*) and helminths (tiny worms, like *Ascaris*, *Taenia* and *Trichinella*). Most of these do not affect the preserved foods dis-cussed here, and can be controlled through the usual methods of proper storage, appropriate cooking temperatures and good sanitation practices.

So far, the organisms we have examined do not cause major problems with the preserved foods with which this book is concerned – despite the fact that they cause most food spoilage and/or food-borne illnesses. In the next examples, we will meet some of the nasty organisms about which we should definitely be concerned.

Escherichia coli, or simply *E. coli*, is the primary species of bacteria living in the intestines of warm-blooded animals. Most strains are harmless – in fact, they help us by converting vitamin K, found in plants, to vitamin K_2 (low levels of which are associated with osteoporosis and coronary heart disease), and *E. coli* also helps control populations of other possibly harmful bacteria. Unfortunately, one strain (O157:H7) has attracted a lot of attention as the cause of a shigellosis-like disease. Certain species of the genus *Shigella* (*S. boydii*, *S. dysenteriae*, *S. flexneri* and *S. sonnei*) are so similar to *E. coli* that some taxonomists think that the *Shigella* strains should be considered as strains of *E. coli*. Shigellosis disease is spread by exposure to faecal matter, either in water or through contamination of foodstuffs during processing, and can be controlled by thorough cooking and good sanitation. As few as ten cells of O157:H7 can multiply rapidly and produce a cytotoxin (verotoxin, or VT) that attacks the cells that line the intestines, causing haemorrhagic colitis – classic dysentery. The disease begins as abdominal cramping and loose diarrhoea, then progresses to bloody diarrhoea. This bacterial infection – not to be confused with amoebic dysentery – is serious and deadly: it killed over 80,000 Union soldiers during the American Civil War.

One of the disturbing aspects of O157:H7 is how it gets to us. When an animal carcase is exposed to faecal matter, the meat from that animal is not always isolated. Ground beef from dozens of animals is sometimes mixed and distributed – nationwide or even worldwide – before anyone knows about the problem. This type of contamination has led to recalls of thousands of pounds of ground beef – not always before it reaches consumers. According to the

Centers for Disease Control and Prevention, *E. coli* sickens some 76,000 people each year in the U.S. alone. O157:H7 can be especially dangerous when the meat is used in uncooked sausages, like salami, that are normally consumed raw.

Now we come to *Clostridium botulinum* (and its related species *C. butyricum* and *C. baratii*), the bacteria that causes botulism. If there is anything that generates panic in consumers of preserved foods, it is botulism. Eating foods contaminated with these *Clostridium* species leads to paralysis and sometimes death, usually due to respiratory failure. Perhaps because of that well-deserved dread, cases of food-borne botulism are fairly rare – roughly twenty per year in the U.S. The related *C. perfringens* causes only diarrhoea and abdominal cramping, symptoms which are still nothing one wishes to experience, even if they are not life-threatening. The bacteria themselves do not cause botulism, but they produce the botulinum toxin (BTX or BONT), which is so potent that its effects can be initiated by a dose as small as a few nanograms – mere billionths of a gram. Under preferred conditions, the spores multiply rapidly, producing the neurotoxins that cause botulism. Once ingested, their victim can experience symptoms such as blurred or double vision, difficulty swallowing, drooping eyelids, dry mouth, muscle weakness or slurred speech in as little as six hours, though eighteen to 36 hours is more common. In rare cases the symptoms might not show up for ten days, making it difficult to determine which food was responsible.

Clostridium spores exist in soil and in the digestive systems of fish and mammals, where it can easily contaminate the foods we might want to preserve in cans or jars. The bad news for preservers is that *Clostridium* is anaerobic, thriving in low-oxygen environments – exactly like the inside of a jar. Fortunately for home preservers, two strategies exist to prevent *Clostridium*'s survival in preserved food: the bacteria do not survive well in foods that are high in sugar (such as jams and jellies) or acids (pickles and tomatoes), and they can be killed by long exposure to high temperatures, as in pressure canners. Foods that are low in acid, having a pH above 4.6, or in sugar, or are high in protein, are especially hospitable to *Clostridium*, and should always be treated with the utmost caution. According to the Food and Drug Administration, botulinum toxin's neurotoxins have been found in canned vegetables, such as asparagus, beetroot, corn, green beans, mushrooms, olives, peppers and spinach; prepared foods, like soups and stews; and especially protein-rich foods, like chicken, ham, liver pâté, luncheon meats, sausage and seafood, such as clams, oysters, salmon and tuna.

While some spoilage is easily recognizable by off-colours, textures or smells, this is not always the case. Botulinum-laced food may seem normal, and the seal on the jar may be sound, but if the spores were not killed by adequate time and temperature in a pressure canner, eating it could have disastrous results. Also, the belief that long cooking can render any food safe for consumption is mistaken, since botulinum's toxins are not destroyed by heat.

Even in the absence of spoilage-inducing organisms, foods can 'go bad' on their own. Exposure to oxygen in the air can cause changes in colour, flavour or aroma. It can also cause fats to become rancid. Also, all living things contain a number of enzymes that begin to digest them shortly after death. This natural decomposition is one of the processes that food preservers try to forestall, except when we employ enzymes to 'decompose' some foods into forms we prefer.

Why does a book for foodies spend so much time on such unpleasant subjects as food spoilage and food-borne disease? The reason is that this knowledge is important to an understanding of the methods used in food preservation, and it is useful to recognize some of the characteristics of food spoilage. No one wants to become ill (let alone die) from our preserved foods; nor do we want to waste the foods we have so carefully prepared. A little fear can be a useful thing. This, therefore, might be a

The Admirable and Most Famous Snail Water (1671)

Take a peck of garden shell snails, wash them well in small beer, and put them in a hot Oven till they have done making a noise, then take them out, and wipe them well from the green froth that is upon them, and bruise them shells and all in a stone Mortar, then take a quart of earth worms, scower them with salt, slit them & wash them well with water from their filth, and in a stone Mortar beat them to pieces, then lay in the bottom of your distilled pot Angelica two handfuls, and two handfuls of Celandine upon them, to which put two quarts of Rosemary flowers, Bears foot, Agrimony, red Dock Roots, Bark of Barberries, Betony, Wood sorrel, of each two handfuls, Rue one handful; then lay the Snails and worms on the top of the Herbs and Flowers, then pour on three Gallons of the strongest Ale, and let it stand all night, in the morning put in three ounces of Cloves beaten, six penniworth of beaten Saffron and on the top of them six ounces of shaved Harts-horn, then set on the Limbeck, and close it with paste, and so receive the water by pints, which will be nine in all, the first is the strongest, whereof take in the morning two spoonfuls in four spoonfuls of small Beer, and the like in the afternoon; you must keep a good Diet and use moderate exercise to warm the blood. This Water is good against all Obstructions whatsoever. It cureth a Consumption and Dropsie, the stopping of the Stomach and Liver. It may be distilled with milk for weak people and children, with Harts-tongue and Elecampance.[3]

How to Keep Wine from Sowring (1671)

Tye a piece of very salt Bacon on the inside of your barrel, so as it touch not the Wine, which will preserve Wine from sowring.[4]

good time to discuss a few fallacies about food preservation. Many old receipt books included cures – or, at least, medicines – to deal with diseases and ailments of all sorts, both real and imagined. The 'Rx' on pharmacy signs is the Latin abbreviation for 'receipts' or 'recipes'. Most of those receipts are outside of our topic, but the boundaries between recipes and prescriptions are not always clear – some old recipes are for things we would no longer consider to be medicines. Cordials, for example, were once believed to have curative effects on the heart. They still warm our hearts, but in a very different way. On the other hand, just perusing this recipe from an anonymous book, *A Queens Delight; Or, The Art of Preserving, Conserving and Candying*, would probably achieve the desired outcome: it is difficult to imagine that an 'obstruction' that could stand in the face of a dose of 'admirable and most famous Snail Water'.

One of the most common fallacies is that salt is bad for us. While for certain people – those with high blood pressure, for example – too much salt should be avoided, most of us simply excrete excess salt with no adverse health effects.

Another misconception is that pork must be cooked until grey and virtually dessicated. This belief is perpetuated out of fear of trichinosis (and perhaps salmonellosis). *Trichinae*-infested pork is unusual in modern times; commercially raised pigs rarely have an opportunity to consume meat, the source of the tiny worms. Eating the meat of wild game – bears and boars – has caused a few reported cases. Also, *Salmonella* and *Trichinae* can be killed by cooking the meat to just 55°C (135.5°F). They are also eliminated by thorough curing, so there is little reason to be concerned about the raw pork in salami.

We often read that garlic and some spices have strong anti-microbial effects, and some of us believe that will be enough to protect us from food poisoning. If we act on this belief, however, we are in for a very unpleasant shock. In fact, back in the 1980s, several people contracted botulism from commercially jarred garlic in oil. As a result, the FDA has required, since 1989, that all forms of commercial garlic-in-oil be prepared with an acidifying agent (typically either citric or phosphoric acids).

TWO

Ancient Preserving Methods

*T*he previous chapter may have led you to believe that only rigorous scientific monitoring of the entire food-preservation process can save you from excruciatingly painful disease symptoms and a gruesome death, but it is reassuring to know that people have safely preserved their foods for thousands of years – entire millennia before science even existed. Granted, there must have been some catastrophic failures, but the survivors created a legacy of safe practices, even if they did not understand the mechanisms responsible for their success.

Drying

Drying was probably the first method discovered by our culinary ancestors. It is easy to imagine an early hunter-gatherer finding that food left inadvertently on a sunny rock had dried out before it had a chance to spoil. We know that people were purposely drying and storing food in Asia and in the Middle East 14,000 years ago. Drying is basically a stalling technique. By slowing down the rate of spoilage, we are able to eat the food before fungi and bacteria get the chance. Drying food preserves its nutrients by making it inhospitable to agents of decay. Evaporation removes water from thinly cut foods by increasing their surface to volume ratio, leaving the interior with insufficient moisture for organisms to multiply enough to become dangerous.

Dried squid in a Chinese market in Bangkok. Thais fry it and then add it to a tart salad of coriander (cilantro), red onion and shredded green mango, dressed with fish sauce, lime juice, sugar and toasted, powdered chillies.

Drying preserves food by reducing its water activity. Water activity (expressed as 'a_w') is a measure of how effectively water can dissolve other substances, such as the nutrients that feed bacteria and moulds. It varies with temperature, so the warmer the water, the more easily nutrients dissolve and the more effectively organisms can utilize them. That effectiveness is limited only by the temperature at which the enzymes in the organisms are destroyed by heat. The higher the water activity, the more likely that spoilage will occur. Conversely, the lower the number, the drier and safer a food becomes. Bacteria begin to thrive above $a_w 0.91$, while fungi and moulds only flourish above $a_w 0.7$. The right combination of dryness and temperature is needed to preserve food: for example, salami that is safe to store in cool Europe might not last long in the hot, humid tropics.

When the sixteenth-century Jesuit José de Acosta visited the Andes, he observed the ancient Inca drying potatoes, called *ch'uñu*, by exposing them first to the cold dry nights of the altiplano, and then again to the warm daytime sun. The altiplano can get as little as 200 mm (8 inches) of precipitation per year, and this incredibly arid climate in addition to the low air pressure at high altitude made for ideal drying conditions. This method in fact pre-dates the Inca, as the Tiwanaku, a civilization that resided in what is today Bolivia and Peru, began drying potatoes using this method around 400 BCE.

However, drying, as done by the ancients, is not a perfect technique for all situations. Regions that are dry and have good air flow or wind are ideal, but in areas where humidity is commonly high, drying might not be fast enough to outpace the spoilers. Some foods rot before achieving the low moisture content necessary to be safe from microorganisms.

Also, during the drying process, various chemical reactions take place besides mere evaporation. Maillard reactions, which are chemical processes similar to caramelization, but involving proteins and carbohydrates, not just sugars, occur at much lower temperatures; a seared steak browns due to Maillard reactions – it is not, as many food writers and chefs assert, 'caramelized' – causing some browning and creation of secondary flavours. These are not necessarily unpleasant. They often add a desirable complexity and deepening of the food's flavour. Prunes and raisins, for example, have flavour profiles that are very different from those of plums and grapes.

Some flavours in fresh foods are more volatile than others, meaning that as the ingredient dries, the balance of flavours and aromas can change. Fresh tarragon, for example, smells warmly of anise and dill, with a hint of freshly cut grass. Once dried, however, some of the anise and all of the dill will have evaporated away. In addition to the loss of some anethole (the essential oil that provides the anise, or liquorice, flavour), fermentation during drying increases the coumarin, which provides the sweet hay scent. Fresh and dried tarragon are, therefore, two quite different ingredients.

Air-dried meats, like ham or jerky, are long-lasting, but even if they are rehydrated they will never taste the same as when they were fresh. Some of their original compounds are lost or changed, and new ones are developed during the process. They become new ingredients.

Drying serves another useful purpose beyond protecting the food from spoilage; it makes the food lighter and more compact. Evaporation makes it possible to can concentrated versions of foods, such as tomato paste. Distillation can be considered a form of dehydration – one that can literally and figuratively raise our spirits. Sometimes preservatives are added to dried foods, though they may not be necessary if refrigeration or freezing is used as well to guarantee long, safe storage.

Salting

First among the chemical preservatives is salt, sodium chloride. Salting speeds the drying of foodstuffs because salt is hygroscopic; it attracts water like a sponge. A coating of salt pulls water to the surface of a food, from where it can evaporate. The same process also creates an osmotic pressure differential between the inside and outside of the cells of microorganisms, bursting and killing them. Besides adding its own taste, salt serves two other functions: it enhances the flavours of other things, and provides an environment that favours some beneficial bacteria that cause other desirable chemical changes (which will be discussed later).

While salt serves several important functions in food preservation, it also tastes good (and synergistically allows us to better perceive other flavours in our food).

> Ye are the salt of the earth: but if the salt have lost his savour, wherewith shall it be salted? It is thenceforth good for nothing, but to be cast out, and to be trodden under foot of men (Matthew 5:13).

Expressions like 'salt of the earth' reflect our love affair with salt and, as Jesus suggested, metaphorical salt can preserve our souls as well. A linguistic connection exists between words for some things we really, really like: salaries, sauces, salsas and sausages – all of which are derived from the Latin *salsus*, 'salted'. In sausage, salt has three functions: first, it helps preserve perishable meats, killing some bacteria that could cause spoilage. Second, it dissolves a portion of the protein (myosin) in the meats which, when cooked, forms a smooth binding matrix for the bits of meat in the sausage. Sausage makers (or processors) can easily see when soluble proteins have been released by the salt, as the ground meat mixture becomes sticky. The ratio of ingredients necessary for this binding to occur is simple: one ounce of salt to every five pounds of meat (13 g per kilogram). Third, it adds, or enhances, flavour.[1]

The most common form of salt for preserving food is called 'pickling salt'. It is merely a fine-textured salt with no additives. The small size of its particles ensures quick dissolving when making brines, and helps the salt adhere to the sur-faces of air-dried foods, such as bacon or ham. The absence of other chemicals such as anti-caking ingredients prevents clouding or off-flavours. Iodine compounds are essential for human health, but iodized salt should not be used for pickling because it can interfere with the very organisms we employ to ferment our foods.

Fleur de sel, flakes of sea salt from the south of France.

We require salt to stay alive, though perhaps not as much as we get in our modern junk-food diets.

Smoking

Smoking, as a food-preservation method, was probably discovered by early humans who lived in cool climates.

> Smoked foods almost always carry with them legends about their having been created by accident – usually the peasant hung the food too close to the fire, and then, imagine his surprise the next morning when . . .[2]

Meats, fish, cheese and other foods left to hang in their shelters – away from the rain that hindered their speedy desiccation – would have absorbed the smoky air from the hearths. Our ancestors discovered that smoked food not only dried faster, but could be stored for longer without spoiling. Moreover, it had a delicious new flavour.

Smoking, alone or in combination with drying, salting and curing, more effectively preserves foods than the other methods. Phenolic compounds in the smoke particles (such as guaiacol and syringol) produced when wood is burned are toxic to many spoilage organisms, and provide the smoky tastes and aromas we have come to love.

Exclusion of Air

Each of the previous preservation methods produced dried foodstuffs that could be stored, as is, anywhere (at least where rodents and bears could not get to them). Sometime after humans came up with food-storage devices that could hold liquids (dried gourds, animal skin bags, pottery or hollowed-out logs), a whole new range of preserved foods became possible. It is unknown how long ago this occurred, but a recent discovery – a metre-long hollowed-out oak log buried during the Iron Age in an Irish bog – suggests that it was over 3,000 years ago. This 35-kg 'barrel' was filled with butter. The find was unusual in that it still contained recognizable butter, but many other firkins have been found in Irish peat, especially in County Mayo. Iron-age bog-dwellers had discovered that burying an air-tight container of food in a bog kept it safe, although it is unlikely that they had intended to store it for over a thousand years. People also topped up jars with honey, olive oil or melted animal fat, securing the openings with oiled paper, animal skins or bladders. They may not have known what they were hiding their food from, but they were definitely on the right track.

The below recipe for preserved butter still works. The Kikuyu people of Kenya heavily coat roasted meats with honey to preserve them. The resulting slightly fermented flesh, called *rukuri*, can last for days – even in the hot African sun. Indian *ghee* is butter that has been clarified to remove water and milk proteins that might spoil, allowing the pure butterfat to be stored, without refrigeration, for long periods.

Exclusion of air and airborne microorganisms helps to preserve fruit. It also preserves other foods for which sugar might not be appropriate. Fats can exclude air and like sugar can be heated to higher temperatures than water. French *confits* (of duck or goose meat, for example), and some pâtés and terrines, are sealed under a layer of melted fat – or sometimes gelatine – that excludes air from the perishable proteins.

Hannah Woolley's recipe reproduced here is not exactly to modern tastes, but considerably more appealing than her advice

Butter, Preserved with Honey (*c.* 1870)

Wash and press the butter until it is quite free from milk. Put it in a jar, and place it in a pan of boiling water. When clarified, and just before boiling, remove it from the water to a cool place; take off the scum, and work it up in the proportion of two ounces of honey to every two pounds of butter. This mode of preparation will be found very convenient where butter is eaten with sweet dishes. It will keep as long as salted butter if the air be excluded from it.[3]

> ## To Keep Venison Nine or Ten Months Good and Sweet (1664)
>
> Take a haunch of Venison and bore holes in it, then stop in seasoning into it as you do parsley into beef in the inside of it if it be red Deer, take pepper, nutmeg, cloves, mace and salt; if it be fallow deer then only pepper and salt; when it is thus seasoned dip it in white wine vineger, and put it in an earthen pot with the salt side down and having first sprinkled good store of spice into the pot; if it be fallow deer three pound of butter will serve, but if red deer then four pounds; when you put it into the oven lay an earthen dish over it, and paste it close up that no air can get out nor in, so let it stand six or seven hours in a very hot oven; when it is baked take off the cover and put in a trencher and a stone upon it to keep the meat down in the liquor; fill up the pot with melted butter and so keep it.[4]

on 'Venison How to Recover when Tainted' in *The Gentlewoman's Companion; or, a Guide to the Female Sex*, published in 1673: 'Take a clean cloth and wrap your Venison therin, then bury it in the Earth one whole night, and it will take away the ill scent or favour.'[5]

Curing and Fermenting

At first glance, these seem like bad strategies if our goal is to keep microorganisms from consuming human food. Why would we do anything to encourage them to infect food we plan to eat ourselves? And yet, that is exactly what we do.

When we age food, we provide the conditions that certain organisms like, and give them time to consume tiny amounts of our store of food. In exchange, they change the food into something different. As certain bacteria multiply, they produce chemical compounds as waste (alcohols, lactic and acetic acids, and peptides), chemicals that discourage the growth of competing bacteria. Fortunately for us, the losers in that competition are the ones that cause the undesirable spoilage. What's more, we find some of the waste products tasty. Bacterial wastes (lactic and/or acetic acid) not only provide tangy flavours, but lower the pH to a level at which undesirable bacteria (like *C. botulinum*) cannot reproduce. When *Lactococcus lactis* ferments lactose (in milk) or dextrose, it also produces nisin, a compound that inhibits the growth of *B. cereus*, *C. botulinum* and *S. aureus*, as well as the spores of some moulds.

Other species, such as *B. subtilis*, convert various seeds and beans into pungent condiments. Soya beans become Chinese *shuǐdòuchǐ*; Indian *akhuni*, *hawaijaar* and *piak*; Japanese *natto*; Korean *cheonggu-kjang*; Nepalese *kinema*; and Thai *thuanao*. West African soya beans and *néré* seeds (*Parkia biglobosa*) are converted into *dawadawa*, *iru*, *netetou* and *sumbala* – local names for a dried paste used to thicken and flavour soups, like *egusi*. Small balls of this paste keep for months, ready to be reconstituted, as needed, like bouillon cubes; lately, large companies – like Maggi – have marketed such cubes to compete with the indigenous product. *B. subtilis* also ferments oil seeds, such as sesame or watermelon, producing *ogiri*, a rich (and richly odoriferous) seasoning paste.

Boiling the juices from fruits such as apples, plums and grapes kills the micro-organisms that live in the whitish bloom on their skin; when uncooked fruits are crushed, however, their juices are exposed to the airborne yeasts in that bloom, and fermentation occurs. The yeasts feed on sugars in the juice, leaving behind certain waste products that humans like, such as carbon dioxide and ethyl alcohol. If the resulting brew is protected from airborne or insect-borne bacteria, it becomes a relatively stable preserved 'food'. If not, bacteria consume the alcohol, converting it to vinegar.

Moulds can be purposely introduced to curing cheeses, either by injection, as a surface wash, or merely by storing the young cheeses in an environment where spores of the desired species are present. Otherwise bland, firm cheeses are gradually colonized by veins of blue or green mould (Roquefort or Gorgonzola, for example, from *Penicillium roqueforti*), or the cheese develops a velvety, white exterior that gradually consumes part of the cheese's 'paste', making it runny, flavourful and aromatic (as with Brie or Camembert, from *P. candidum*). The bacterial washes used on some cheeses, such as *Brevibacterium linens* on Limburger or *Crottin de Chavignol*, give them a fragrant golden, rusty or even dark greyish-brown rind. Moulds are also responsible for the complex flavours of many soya-based products in Asia.

Over time, a cascade of chemical reactions occur in these infected foods. Each chemical change results in a new environment, in which a variety of reactions and populations of microorganisms are possible. Wines and cheeses are familiar examples of

Rogue River Creamery blue cheese from Central Point, Oregon, showing *Penicillium* mould, and a wrapping of young grape leaves.

this sequence of change, but many other foods exhibit similar development of flavours, aromas and textures.

Ageing is controlled intentional spoilage, in which humans and microorganisms share a symbiotic relationship. Humans and microorganisms are not the only creatures that share such relationships. Lichens, for example, are a team of fungi and algae working together for their mutual benefit, but food preservers use *tibicos*. A *tibicos* is similar to the symbiotic colony of bacteria and yeasts (SCOBY) that forms in fermenting foodstuffs. SCOBYs are usually gelatinous masses, rather like the 'mother of vinegar' that converts wine to acetic acid, while *tibicos* form grain-like lumps that settle to the bottom of *kefir* (a fermented milk drink). The bacterial species include *Acetobacter ketogenum* and *A. xylinum*; *Gluconacetobacter kombuchae*; *Lactobacillus brevis* and other spp.; *Leuconostoc* spp.; *Pediococcus* spp.; and *Streptococcus* spp. Yeast genera commonly involved in these communities include *Brettanomyces*, *Candida*, *Kloeckera*, *Saccharomyces* and the species *Zygosaccharomyces kombuchaensis*. The 'kombucha' in *Z. kombuchaensis* refers to the *tibicos* that produce a fermented sweet tea originally consumed from Japan to Russia, but now popular worldwide.

Pickling

Pickling is another ancient means of preserving food, one that often makes use of some of the biological helpers previously mentioned. Essentially, pickling preserves food by creating an acidic environment that prevents or retards the development of undesirable agents of decomposition.

Our word 'pickle' actually comes from a Dutch word for brine. With cool temperatures and low concentrations of salt, *Leuconostoc mesenteroides* bacteria turn sugars into alcohol and various acids. As the temperature rises, or if initial salt concentrations are higher, *Lactobacillus plantarum* instead produces large amounts of lactic acid,

which effectively prevents other, less desirable bacteria from the future pickles, sauerkraut or kimchi.

Another method is to apply the acid directly to potential pickles. Typically, the acid of choice is vinegar (acetic or ethanoic acid), itself a product of twofold fermentation. Acetic acid can be produced synthetically, but most pickled foods are made with 'natural' vinegars, whose original source was apples or grapes, for example with cider or wine vinegars.

Confitur-ing and Candying

Tianjin preserved vegetable is like a drier version of kimchi; it's chopped cabbage and garlic, heavily salted, then fermented.

Confitures are jams, jellies and similar preserves made with high concentrations of sugars. Originally made with honey, they preserve fruits by a series of methods. The fruits are first juiced, or cut into relatively small pieces, thus increasing the surface to volume ratio, thereby reducing the chance of spoilage in the interior of the fruit. Next, they are cooked at high temperatures, an act made possible by the sugar. Water boils at 100°C (212°F) at sea level, but adding sugar allows higher temperatures. Pure sugar melts at 186°C (367°F), so solutions of sugar in water can achieve maximum temperatures between those of pure water and pure sugar, depending on concentration.

Sugar, like salt, is strongly hygroscopic. It extracts water that might allow undesirable fermentation (decay) of the fruit. Strong solutions of sugars, such as honey, are shelf-stable because they have low water activity. In other words, they do not contain enough water for microorganisms, like bacteria and yeasts, to survive. When foods are impregnated with, and covered by, such thick concentrations of sugar, they have little chance of spoilage.

Like salt, however, sugars can sometimes be overwhelming. Only a child's palate can appreciate the sweetness of unalloyed sugar. Most of the foods preserved with sugar are appealing because that sweetness is played off against other basic tastes: the sourness of acids in fruit preserves, the bitterness of cocoa or coffee in chocolates, a little saltiness, or a combination of all these tastes. We also like to soften the saccharine edge of sugar with the rich mouthfeel of fats. As Marie Antoinette famously never said, 'Let them eat cake!'

Acids

After salt and sugar, acids are probably the most historically significant food-preserving chemicals. Other than the lactic acid produced through fermentation, vinegar is the primary preserving acid. Vinegar is itself a preserved food. When ethyl alcohol is consumed by bacteria (*Acetobacter* species), acetic acid is produced. This is highly undesirable if one's goal is to keep wine as wine. If one does not fancy bottles of very expensive vinegar, a few strategies exist to avoid this. *Acetobacter* requires oxygen to live, so sealing the wine away from air is essential. Open bottles of wine 'go sour' because they have been exposed to air as well as *Acetobacter*. Some oenophiles use a blanket of relatively inert gas (such as nitrogen) in opened bottles to prevent the growth of these bacteria. Winemakers sterilize their equipment and bottles with sulphur dioxide to eliminate contamination.

If, however, one does want to make vinegar, all that is required is an alcohol solution of choice, exposure to air and some time. The bacteria will find it and start building a slimy colony called a 'mother'. The type of vinegar made is determined by the kind of alcoholic beverage used. Wine vinegars can be made from red wine, white wine, rice wine, champagne or sherry – each developing a distinctive flavour and aroma. Malt vinegar, the classic condiment for British fish and chips, is made from beer (the medieval ingredient *alegar* is a malt vinegar). Cider vinegar, as you might suspect by now, is made from cider (hard apple cider), and retains a little of the taste of the orchard. Fermented coconut water becomes *sukang niyog*, a sharp vinegar used in cooking in Sri Lanka, the Philippines and parts of southern India. The Philippines' *sukang iloko* is made from the fermented juice of sugar cane and is named after a region that is famous for its vinegar, even if this particular vinegar is from somewhere else. Sour tastes characterize Filipino cuisine, and cooks make use of a wide spectrum of acidic ingredients in addition to vinegar. In Egypt, Iran and Saudi Arabia, dates yield a thick brown vinegar. Chinese black vinegar (*wu cu* or *hei cu*) is darker still, with a complex, slightly spicy flavour resulting from long fermentation and a variety of grains such as millet, rice, sorghum and wheat. Japanese *kurozu* is similar to *wu cu*, but is made with rice only. It is milder, with a diminished acidic bite.

In Iceland, fermented whey is often used to preserve foods. The whey's high lactic acid content prevents spoilage of ingredients most of us have never encountered, such as seal flippers, whale blubber and the intestines, suet and pressed testicles of lambs, as well as slightly more familiar ones, *blóðmör* (black pudding) and *lifrarpylsa* (a type of liver sausage).

Fats

The importance of fats in food preservation is shown by the very fact that our name for the place where we keep our preserved foods – or did, before the invention of refrigerators – is the 'larder'. Originally, it referred to a room where lard was rendered.

Lard is made by slowly simmering chunks of pork fat (with a little water to get it started, before the fat begins to melt) until all the clear fat has been rendered. At the end, the liquid fat is strained and cooled into pure white blocks of lard. The crisp bits of fried meat and connective tissue that adhered to the original fat are called 'crackling', or, more affectionately, 'cracklins', and are a special treat reserved for those who make their own lard. Pure lard, with no moisture content, keeps very well, though shelf-stable commercially produced lard usually contains BHA and/or BHT, antioxidants that retard rancidity.

The very firm fat taken from around a pig's internal organs yields high quality 'leaf lard'. Leaf lard has not always had the best reputation for purity. In Upton Sinclair's exposé of the meat-packing industry, *The Jungle* (1906), he reported an accident in which a worker fell into a rendering vat and was processed into lard that was later sold to unwitting consumers. Such revelations were in large part responsible for the passage, shortly thereafter, of America's Pure Food and Drug Act.

THREE
Modern Preserving Methods

*T*oday's food industry uses many high-tech methods to preserve food, most of which are beyond the reach of home cooks. Nonetheless, technologies have a habit of working their way down the food chain, so it is not inconceivable that, some day, our home kitchens may contain devices that make use – on a smaller scale, of course – of some of these methods. A hundred years ago, who would have imagined that home kitchens in the twenty-first century would routinely sport food processors, KitchenAids, freezers, Cryovacs and microwave ovens?

Canning

Our ideas of modern food preservation began in 1795, when Nicolas-François Appert, a French chef, noticed that the French Directory was offering a prize of 12,000 francs for a method of preserving food, primarily so that it could be transported along with Napoleon's armies. Since Appert had long been interested in pickling, brewing and distilling, he was uniquely qualified to take on the challenge.

Appert knew that Lazzaro Spallanzani had – nearly three decades earlier, through sterilization with heat – questioned the then-accepted notion that microbes were created by spontaneous generation. Appert realized that his own process would have to address two separate issues: destroying any living things in the

CAN
ALL YOU
CAN

IT'S A REAL WAR JOB!

OWI Poster No. 77 — 7½" x 10½". Additional copies may be obtained upon request from the Division of Public Inquiries, Office of War Information, Washington, D. C.   ☆ U. S. GOVERNMENT PRINTING OFFICE : 1943—O—533093

Nicolas-François
Appert on a com-
memorative postage
stamp issued in
recognition of the
200th anniversary
of the invention of
canning (July 2010).

"L'appertisation"

1810 : Nicolas Appert rend publique son invention

food, and preventing new ones from getting back in afterwards. He spent the next fourteen years trying different methods of heating and sealing, before finally succeeding. His method involved the use of an autoclave – essentially a pressure cooker that could reach temperatures well above the boiling point of water – to accomplish the sterilization.

His trick for solving the second issue of keeping new microbes out was ingenious. Loosely corked glass jars or bottles of food were covered with water in the autoclave. As the food was heated past the boiling point, it was sterilized and steam and air were pushed past the loose corks. The covering of boiling water prevented anything from re-entering the bottles. When the processing was complete, the corks were pushed in tightly and the tops were bound with wire and sealed with wax.

In 1811 he published his results in *L'Art de conserver, pendant plusieurs années, toutes les substances animals et végétales* (The Art of Preserving All Kinds of Animal and Vegetable Substances for Several Years). He used his winnings to establish La Maison Appert, the world's first cannery. It continued to operate at Massy, in the

U.S. Second World War propaganda, urging home food preservation in support of the war effort. In 1943 alone, American home cooks put up over four billion jars of home-grown vegetables.

southern suburbs of Paris, until 1933. Today's home bottling is, in principle, the same as Appert's.

Appert himself never fully appreciated the reason why his method worked. Despite his success, and Spallanzani's original research, the scientific community was still divided on the issue of spontaneous generation almost 100 years later. Scientists like Georges-Louis Leclerc (more familiarly known to us as the Comte du Buffon) were not convinced; they believed that the heat of Spallanzani's experiments had somehow destroyed an unknown 'vegetative force' that scientists imagined must exist – a concept long since discredited, like the ether, phlogiston and animal magnetism.

Modern industrial canning has evolved in several ways from the methods of Appert and home preservers. Glass jars sturdy enough to withstand the temperatures and pressures of preserving are both heavy and fragile, and so these were soon replaced

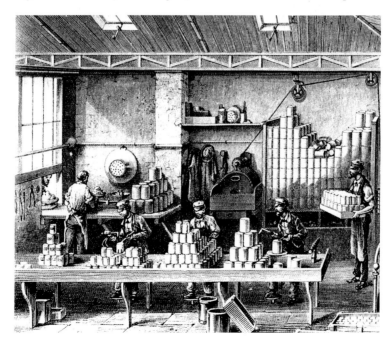

A 19th-century canning factory. Note the men in the foreground using torches to solder lids onto the cans.

by iron cans. These early cans were plated with tin on the inside to prevent acids in the contents from reacting with, and eroding, the iron (which affected first the quality and later the security of the canned food). Lead-tin solder sealed the lids. A famous consequence of using such lead-sealed cans occurred in Britain's Franklin Expedition, which departed England in 1845 in search of a Northwest Passage to Asia. This was the first major attempt to bring along modern canned food on a sea voyage; the party carried enough food for three years at sea. Unfortunately, poorly soldered cans led to lead poisoning, especially among the officers, who had access to the 'best' food. The expedition never got past Hudson's Bay, and the last survivors wound up cannibalizing each other.

Two important technological innovations made the canning industry possible: Appert's invention of the autoclave, of course, but also the discovery that adding certain salts can raise the normal boiling point of water from 100°C (212°F). A saturated solution of ordinary salt could raise it up to 108°C (227°F), while one of calcium chloride could increase it to 170°C (338°F). By 1861 a canner in Baltimore, Maryland, had already decreased processing times to one-twelfth of those of the methods employing autoclaves.

Early 'tin cans' were made of heavy gauge steel and were so difficult to open that a cook had to use a hammer and chisel. Just in time for America's Civil War, lighter-weight cans made can-opening devices practical. The first self-opening cans – like the ones still found on sardine tins and some coffee cans – followed a decade later. Canned beer went on the market in 1935, soon after Prohibition ended. The early beer cans had cone-shape tops and screw caps. Later, flat-topped beer cans led to the invention of a leveraged puncturing tool that gripped the can's edge for a fulcrum – the 'church key'. Self-opening beer and soda cans – 'pop tops' – were invented in the U.S. in 1959, but were phased out, because users would create litter by discarding the pull-up rings, when the Sta-tab was introduced in 1975.

Today's 'tin cans' no longer contain tin, nor are they soldered shut. The inner surfaces of steel cans are plated with various metals (aluminium, chromium and nickel), plus phosphates and some polymers. The lids are sealed with an overlapping inter-locked seam, much like the ones seen on blue jeans, with a flexible thermoplastic resin as cement. Many of these cans are now made of aluminium, which is lighter and less susceptible to corrosion. Pressurized contents (beer or soft carbonated drinks) help thinner cans keep their shape, saving both weight and cost. Lightweight plastics (low- and high-density polyethylenes, polyethylene ter-aphthalate, polypropylene, polystyrene, polyvinylchloride and various composites) have largely replaced glass jars and bottles. These plastics have different properties – for example, poly-ethylene terephthalate has the highest clarity, making it ideal for revealing the colour and crystalline quality of oils. Additionally, non-composite plastics can be recycled.

In 1869 Henry John Heinz began packing foods in jars. He sold jars of grated horseradish, using his mother's recipe, in Sharpsburg, Pennsylvania. As public concern over food safety and sanitation grew, largely in response to Upton Sinclair's exposé of the meatpacking industry, Heinz cap-italized on that concern by shipping his products in clear, colourless glass jars and promoting them as 'altogether pure food'. His company sold a huge variety of jarred goods, including baked beans, ketchup, mincemeat, mustard, olives, pepper sauces, pickles (of several kinds, including cauliflower and onions), soups, sauerkraut and vinegar. Today, many Heinz products are still shipped in clear jars and bottles, though they are more likely seen through plastic than glass.

Hop flavouring can label, c. 1921. Since this product was sold during Prohibition, its label includes a required warn-ing: 'Do not use for making intoxicating beverages.' That was at least disingenuous, and possibly tongue-in-cheek, since hops are rarely used for anything else.

Technological Innovations of the Nineteenth Century

Appert's invention of canning in 1810 was quickly followed by other innovations. His method, using glass jars, was widely published and shortly thereafter Peter Durand began filling containers made of tin-plated steel in England. Durand held the patent, but did not come up with the idea; that credit belongs to a French inventor, Philippe de Girard. De Girard wanted to patent it in England, but since the two countries were involved in a conflict known in America as 'the War of 1812', part of the much larger Napoleonic Wars being fought all over Europe, he could not use his own name. The American food-packer William Underwood coined the term 'cans'. It was in widespread use by 1839, although in Britain the term 'cans' never replaced 'tins'.

While Underwood's grandson, William Lyman Underwood, ran the family business in 1895, he worried about the problem of bulging canned clams. Clearly, something was wrong with their processing, but he couldn't determine the reason. He took his problem to Professor William Thompson Sedgwick at the Massachusetts Institute of Technology. Sedgwick passed the problem along to a 24-year-old instructor, Samuel Cate Prescott. Prescott found that not all parts of a can's contents were reaching safe temperatures, allowing heat-resistant bacterial spores to survive the canning process. He also learned that holding the cans at 121°C (250°F) for ten minutes ensured a safe product. Prescott and Underwood continued to work together until the latter's death in 1929, identifying other food-spoilage bacteria, and methods for disabling them. In an ethical gesture, 'neither of the scientists, nor the William Underwood Company, filed for patents on their methods, which they hoped would improve food safety for all consumers.'[1]

The fin de siècle was the golden age of mechanical labour-saving devices, marking the beginning of mass-produced food preservation. We have already seen the impact of improvements to transportation. But with expanding urban populations and mechanically enhanced agriculture (using inventions such as John Deere's steel plough and Cyrus McCormick's mechanical reaper), the mass-production of preserved foods was needed more than ever before.

The packing plant of Chicago's nineteenth-century meat magnate P. D. Armour was a great example of mechanical ingenuity. He also added ice-chilled rooms that more than doubled the length of the packing season.

> Armour's use of emerging technologies, in both processing and transportation, was among his most important contributions. Armour was one of the first to develop a processing line (a precursor of Ford's assembly line – or, in Armour's case, a disassembly line) to prepare the carcasses of hogs.[2]

The invention of the telegraph allowed men like Armour to take advantage of meat and feed futures, and to negotiate contracts with the Union Army, which purchased nearly 700 million pounds of salted meat during the Civil War. Once cities began to be electrified, and artificial refrigeration replaced ice, the market for salted meats largely disappeared. Today, the primary salted meats are bacon, ham and sausage – with small amounts of salt pork and fatback, used mainly for seasoning.

While preservation techniques were originally devised to ensure adequate food supplies during lean times, modern industrialization created a new and different problem: huge surpluses, much more than existing markets could bear. This meant that producers, for the first time, had to manufacture demand for all of that excess. The best way to accomplish this was through advertising. The first American ad agency was N. W. Ayer & Son, founded in Philadelphia in 1869, which created Morton Salt's 'When it rains, it pours' campaign in 1912. The ads displayed in this book would never have existed were it not for the overproduction made possible by the mechanization and transportation systems of the nineteenth century.

Condensing

During the American Civil War, the military's need for reliably transportable foodstuffs led to other food preservation discoveries. Two men made it their business to give the armies what they needed: Gail Borden and Philip Danforth Armour.

Appert had dehydrated beef broth into something resembling bouillon cubes in 1831 and by 1849, Borden started experimenting with condensing beef broth. He added flour to make a long-lasting protein-rich ration marketed to the U.S. Army as 'beef biscuit pemmican'. The explorer Edwin de Haven carried them along on two Arctic explorations, in 1850 and 1853, while searching for the lost Franklin Expedition. De Haven's explorers, unlike Franklin's, returned alive, although many suffered from scurvy – Borden's biscuits lacked vitamin C. Borden tried to market his beef biscuits to a wider public, but they didn't sell. Perhaps they required a captive audience, or at least diners who had fewer menu choices available. Nearly bankrupt, but undiscouraged, Borden changed his focus to a different food.

Before refrigeration, whole milk was too perishable for consumption in urban areas. Furthermore, another form of consumption (tuberculosis) also discouraged the drinking of milk. Today, pasteurization and government oversight of the dairy industry have largely eliminated the milk-TB problem; however,

> One infant . . . died and dozens of New Yorkers have contracted tuberculosis from 2001 through 2004 by eating cheese made from raw milk that was contaminated with bacteria, city and federal officials said yesterday.

[New York] city's Department of Health and Mental Hygiene warned that several types of cheese imported from Mexico, particularly queso fresco, might be contaminated with Mycobacterium bovis, which causes tuberculosis.[3]

Borden had heard about the death of several children who had insufficient or tainted milk on a sea voyage, and became obsessed with finding a way to concentrate milk, safely, while preserving its taste. However, Borden did not understand the chemistry of milk – he believed it was alive, and 'as soon as drawn from the cow, begins to die, change, and decompose'.[4] He understood that reducing its water content by cooking would not work. Once milk proteins have been heated beyond 82°C (180°F), they are denatured – the milk curdles and cannot be restored to its original smooth liquid form; indeed, Appert had made an unsatisfactory version of condensed milk in 1820 using that method. Once Borden saw a kind of vacuum pan used by Quakers to condense fruit juices, he believed it could be the answer. In 1853 he secured a patent for canned condensed milk that was shelf-stable and pathogen free.

While he managed to find backers for his new company, his first two factories failed. His third attempt, in 1858, was the New York Condensed Milk Company (renamed 'The Borden Company' in 1919). The Civil War created an instant market for Borden's canned milk. Borden continued experimenting with preserving other foods, getting a patent for concentrated fruit juices in 1868. He had once boasted, 'I mean to put a potato in a pillbox, a pumpkin into a tablespoon . . . The Turks made acres of roses into attar of roses . . . I intend to make attar of everything.'[5]

A Borden competitor, Elbridge Amos Stuart, founded a company in 1899 that eventually became the Carnation Evaporated Milk Company. The popularity of evaporated milk is clear from this bit of doggerel that began circulating around the turn of the century:

U.S. Second World War propaganda urging home food preservation. Wars have provided the incentive for much of the progress in food preservation.

"We'll have lots to eat this winter, won't we Mother?"

Grow your own
Can your own

OWI Poster No. 55.   Additional copies may be obtained upon request from the Division of Public Inquiries, Office of War Information, Washington, D.C.

Carnation Milk is the best in the land
Here I sit with a can in my hand
No tits to pull, no hay to pitch
You just punch a hole in the son of a bitch.

Pasteurization

In the second half of the nineteenth century, the French scientist Louis Pasteur worked to resolve the spontaneous generation question. He noticed that fermentation (both bacterial and fungal) could occur even without oxygen, but it proceeded much more rapidly when exposed to the open air. Suspecting that airborne bacteria and yeasts were involved, he exposed sterilized liquids to both open air and to carefully filtered air. He learned that spoilage was much more rapid in the unfiltered air. The concept of spontaneous generation was dead.

Pasteur's work on fermentation and subsequent development of pasteurization led to beer, milk, vinegar and wine becoming stable long-lasting products. Pasteur found that long exposure of foods to high temperatures was often unnecessary and it undesirably affected the quality of some foods, as cooking, itself, altered their flavours. A brief exposure to temperatures of 50–60°C (122–140°F), followed by a quick chill, provided adequate protection for foods with relatively short shelf-lifes, such as refrigerated milk, but would not be safe against *C. botulinum* or for foods with longer storage periods.

Modern pasteurization is available in two methods of processing: high-temperature, short-time (HTST) and ultra-high temperature (UHT). Despite their names, neither process is hot nor lasting enough to cook the milk, though some people can taste the difference with UHT cream. HTST heats milk to 72°C (161°F) for fifteen seconds, while UHT heats it to 138°C (280°F) for at least two seconds. Milk and other dairy products are not the only foods that are pasteurized. Wines were the first to be pasteurized, by

Pasteur himself. Others include canned food, fruit juices, soft or low-alcohol beverages, syrups, vinegars and even water.

Freezing

Most of the meat consumed by the Union and Confederate armies was shipped in the form of heavily salted slabs packed in barrels. Union soldiers disparaged it as 'embalmed beef', though it was more often pork (beef did not become America's primary meat until after the war, when railroads, the mechanization of packing plants, refrigeration and westward expansion led to the possibility of huge herds of open-range cattle being available to eastern cities). P. D. Armour, whose company had produced much of that 'embalmed beef', saw the end of the war approaching and sold his entire inventory of salt pork for $40 a barrel. He then sat back and watched the market collapse, and bought it all back for $5 a barrel. He used the profits to move his plant to Chicago.

However, Gustavus Franklin Swift's refrigerated railcars, beginning in 1881, largely eliminated the market for salted meats. Aside from bacon, most of the salted meat sold still makes use of canning technologies. In 1878 J. A. Wilson invented a tapered can that allowed canned meat to slide out in one large piece. Canned meats served many in the days before home refrigerators were common, but today relatively few meats, primarily hams and potted meats such as Spam, come in cans.

While drying, salting, curing and canning had the ability to preserve foods longer than even the refrigeration in use at the end of the nineteenth century, they were all limited by the fact that the foods were altered in the process of preserving them. In some cases, the alteration was not objectionable – pickles or ketchup are not exactly foods one might have experienced fresh from the garden, so did not suffer from the comparison. But other foods were noticeably different: canned peas could never be mistaken for fresh. In some cases, the loss of quality was more than compensated for by the convenience of having seasonable vegetables year-round, at a reasonable cost. For a long time, canned peas were much more familiar than fresh. They came to be expected; many people had never even seen fresh peas, so they did not regret the loss of quality.

Late nineteenth-century refrigeration technologies made it possible to freeze foods, but shoppers were unimpressed by their poor quality. Clarence Birdseye worked for the U.S. Agriculture Department and, between 1912 and 1915, his job took him to Labrador, Canada. While there, he noticed that the Inuit were freezing fish and seal meat and that their quality was noticeably better than any frozen foods he had sampled at home. He suspected that their success might have something to do with the very low Arctic temperatures, temperatures not used in refrigeration techniques in the U.S.

Some ionic salts, when dissolved, are able not only to raise the boiling point of water, but to lower its freezing point. It is for this reason that such salts are spread on roadways to help remove ice. In 1923 Birdseye realized that he might be able to use that principle to freeze foods as quickly as the Inuit of Labrador had done. Using a cheap electric fan, some ice and a lot of salt, he packed fresh food in small, heavily waxed cardboard boxes, thereby inventing the flash-freezing process. He found that frozen fish and vegetables (like peas and corn) were practically indistinguishable from their fresh counterparts. Six years later, he sold his patents and his name – to a company that later became General Foods in the U.S. – for $22 million.

Like Appert before him, Birdseye probably did not know why his frozen foods were so much better than previous attempts – but he was right that speed was the key difference. When food freezes, its water forms crystals. The more slowly it freezes, the larger the crystals grow. Large crystals exert enough force on the surrounding food to break up the food's tissue structure, destroying the food's texture. Birdseye's low temperatures and small-volume packaging reduced the freezing time, and kept the ice crystals tiny.

Birdseye's idea of packing in heavily waxed containers was also fortuitous. Food kept frozen over a long period gradually loses water through sublimation. This occurs when matter goes from solid to gas (or gas to solid) without passing through a liquid phase. When it happens to frozen foods, their surfaces become dehydrated, resulting in an unpleasant characteristic called 'freezer burn'. By carefully sealing food in those little waxed boxes, Birdseye effectively prevented sublimation of its water. It is no accident that frozen foods still come packed in small, waxed boxes or vapour-proof plastic.

While sublimation often destroys the quality of the food, it can be beneficial as well. It is the key to the process known as 'freeze-drying'. Freeze-drying creates a storable product that can last indefinitely, and is easily restored by rehydrating (some instant coffees are probably the most familiar freeze-dried products). It is accomplished by increasing the surface to volume ratio of the

Frozen foods at the Real Canadian Superstore in Winkler, Manitoba.

food, then exhausting all the air while lowering the temperature. This quickly removes all of the water from the food. Since freeze-drying is more expensive than other drying techniques, such as vaporizing in moving hot air, or spraying onto heated metal surfaces, a combination of methods is sometimes employed.

Partly because of the speed of freeze-drying, some of the undesirable characteristics of other dried foods – off-flavours due to fermentation, oxidation and/or Maillard reactions – are avoided. Freeze-dried foods are commonly used by backpackers, for whom weight is an important factor, and the fruit that comes packed in some cold breakfast cereals is also freeze-dried. Early meals for astronauts were also mostly freeze-dried, but did not rehydrate well. Today's astronauts enjoy meals that utilize a wide range of techniques, including irradiated 'fresh' meats (that, ironically, are not yet approved for Earth-bound consumers in the U.S.). The space station has room for luxuries that were impossible on early missions: refrigerated fresh foods and even an Italian-made espresso machine.

Chemical Additives

'Doctoring' food with chemical preservatives is often seen as a modern form of adulteration, a culinary crime against nature. The mere mention of 'chemicals' sends shivers of horror up the spines (or down the gullets) of those of us who care about what we eat. But what do we really mean by that word?

Everything in the universe, everything we eat – indeed, everything that we are – is made of chemicals. We must eat chemicals to live. The thing that concerns us is not actually the fact that they are chemicals, but that we perceive them as unnatural chemicals – compounds that are not normally part of the wholesome, 'natural' foods we choose to eat. So, let us focus our attention on the chemicals we add to our foods in order to preserve them.

We have already discussed salt, but what non-scientists call 'salt' is only one example of an entire class of chemicals. All salts are the product of a reaction between an acid and a base (sodium chloride, for example, is the product of sodium hydroxide – lye – and hydrochloric acid). Several salts are routinely employed in food preservation. Naturally occurring saltpetre (potassium nitrate) has served, historically, as a preservative for meats. Today, saltpetre has been largely replaced by Peru saltpetre (sodium nitrate) and a similar salt, sodium nitrite, both of which inhibit the growth of dangerous bacteria, such as *Clostridium botulinum*, and inhibit the tendency of fat to become rancid.

Makers of bacon, hams and sausage use nitrite in the form of 'Tinted Cure Mix' (its pink colour distinguishes it from ordinary salt). Also known as Instacure #1, TCM is just salt combined with sodium nitrite ($NaNO_2$), and is the preferred cure for cooked meats that do not require long storage. Instacure #2 is the same thing, but with added sodium nitrate ($NaNO_3$). It is used for uncooked or cold-smoked meats that require longer storage. Both curing salts work by producing nitric oxide (NO_2) gas, which kills spoilage bacteria. $NaNO_2$ releases NO_2 when nitrite's supply of nitric oxide is used up. That is why Instacure #2 is preferred for uncooked, longer-lasting meat products. As an aside, the ruddy colouration in cooked ham is a result of NO_2's reaction with the pigmented proteins, haemoglobin and myoglobin, within the meat. Nitrites have been found to produce dangerous levels of carcinogenic nitrosamines when heated to 130°C (266°F) – a temperature that can be reached when frying bacon until crispy. However, most packagers add vitamin C (L-ascorbic acid), which stops the creation of nitrosamines.

Citric acid – usually in the form of its salt, sodium citrate – is an antioxidant. It slows or eliminates the browning that naturally occurs when some fruits and vegetables are exposed to air – even in the minute quantities present in processed preserving jars. This form of browning is not harmful, but is less appetizing than the bright colours of fresh fruits. Home preservers often use some form of citric or ascorbic acid, either as a synthetic powder, or as a couple of squeezes of lemon juice.

Alum (potassium alum, or hydrated potassium aluminium sulphate), an astringent salt, has a 'tightening' effect on a few different foods. It can be used as a curdling agent to make tofu from soybean 'milk', is sometimes added to vinegar pickles to maintain their crispness and also hardens gelatine.

Caustic soda (or lye, sodium hydroxide) is not chemically a salt, and would seem to be one of the last things we would want to put in our food. However, it does have its culinary uses. We have seen that it makes hominy of dried corn, but it also helps gelatinize starches, which gives pretzels their glossy surface and deep brown colour. Lye serves another purpose in the kitchen, at least in some traditional Scandinavian kitchens. *Lutefisk* begins as dried fish – generally cod, but also haddock, ling or pollock – which may or may not have been salted. The fish is first rehydrated, then soaked in a strongly alkaline solution usually consisting of lye, but which could be – especially in Finland – a slurry of ashes from birch logs. The result is an odoriferous and gelatinous mass that must be washed several times before being cooked. It can be prepared several ways, but no matter which is chosen, the result generally horrifies non-Scandinavians. It is probably no accident that even *lutefisk* lovers prefer to wash it down with glasses of Akvavit.

We have something of a love/hate relationship with the chemistry of commercial foodstuffs, so let us look at some of the chemicals employed specifically to resist spoilage, to extend shelf-lifes or preserve the colour, flavour, smell and texture of mass-produced foods. Most of these chemicals, however, are not used in home food preservation.

Some additives serve only aesthetic purposes, whether as bleaching agents, colourings, flavourings or texture enhancers (such as gelatine, agar agar and various gums). Others – like dough conditioners, emulsifiers and emulsion stabilizers (lecithin, mono- and di-glycerides, or propylene glycol alginate) – are of use only to large-scale producers. For our purposes, we can ignore them. However, we should not ignore some of the other chemicals either in, or involved in the production of, preserved foods. In addition to naturally occurring acids – like lactic and acetic acids – several other acidic compounds are added to foods, including various benzoates, sorbates and sulphites (such as potassium metabisulphite, which preserves their natural colour and inhibits the growth of bacteria). To prohibit the growth of mould, breads frequently contain calcium or sodium propionate and/or sodium diacetate. Butylated hydroxyanisole (BHA) and butylated hydroxytoluene (BHT) are antioxidants that prevent fats from turning rancid. These are often added to products, for example crackers or potato crisps, that contain fats, as well as to the fats themselves, such as cooking oils and lard.

Compounds that prevent changes in a food's appearance, colour, flavour or texture are classed as 'sequestering agents'. Sugar, salt and vinegar act as sequestering agents, but a host of others are employed in commercially preserved foodstuffs. Calcium, potassium and sodium salts of various acids (citric, pyrophosphoric and tartaric) are added to dairy products to deter souring. Ethylenediaminetetraacetic acid (EDTA) prevents liquids from becoming cloudy when exposed to metals, and so is used to store soft drinks in cans. Furthermore, exposing dried fruits to sulphur dioxide gas prevents their browning.

Calcium chloride is used in brewing beer because it aids yeasts during fermentation by improving enzymatic reactions, speeding the metabolism of sugars into alcohol, and because it helps to coagulate proteins in the wort, causing them to settle out and making the beer clearer. In cheese-making, it is important to have the right calcium and protein balance in the milk's casein, so calcium chloride is added when making Brie and Stilton, among other cheeses. It also helps preserved foods retain their firmness (such as for 'firm tofu'). Alum does the same thing for commercial and homemade pickles.

The chemicals listed above are classified as GRAS (generally regarded as safe) by the U.S. government. Other countries may have different standards. The decision to include or not include foods containing these chemicals in our diets is a personal one, for which it is useful to know what they are and why they are used. We should also be careful not to confuse them with similar-sounding chemicals that actually are dangerous.

Irradiation

Irradiation can be used to kill pathogens in food. It does this by breaking the chemical bonds in the cells of living matter. In high enough doses, irradiation kills bacteria, viruses and protozoa, as well as larger creatures, such as insects.

Foods typically preserved by irradiation include fruits, certain meats and spices. Fruits – such as strawberries, papayas and some citrus fruits – are irradiated in part to retard spoilage, but primarily to avoid spreading fruit flies to other agricultural areas. These tiny flies can either damage crops or cause the harvested fruit to deteriorate more quickly. In the United States, irradiation is also employed to keep ground beef and poultry fresh for longer.

Dried herbs and spices are more heavily irradiated than other foods for two reasons. Since they are not washed before use, they are not sprayed with pesticides, leaving the possibility of insect infestations. Also, since these foods are used in such small quantities, even if residual radiation was an issue, consumers' exposure to it is insignificant enough to cause harm. The mere mention of irradiation frightens many people. This is an understandable fear since, while radiation is imperceptible, the sickness it causes is horrible. A little explanation of irradiation, however, may help to reduce some of those fears.

'Radiation' refers to electromagnetic energy in the form of waves; for example, light and radio waves. However, these have little negative effect on us because they have relatively long wavelengths: the shorter the wavelength, the higher the frequency, and the more energy produced – hence the greater effect it can have on the molecules that make up all living matter. We get sunburn, and possibly skin cancers, from exposure to certain frequencies of ultraviolet light because their wavelengths are shorter – more energetic – than visible light. As the frequencies become shorter, they progress through the ranges of X-rays all the way to gamma rays, which are the most dangerous to living cells. There are worse forms of radiation – cosmic rays from outer space, for example – but they are almost entirely blocked by the earth's magnetic field, and are therefore not a threat to the human population (at least, to those of us who are not astronauts). For those of us not wandering about in outer space, there are two concerns: the radiation itself, and materials that emit that radiation.

Exposure to some forms of short-wavelength radiation (such as gamma rays and X-rays) in high enough doses damages our cells and the genetic material within them, leading to radiation sickness, cancers and birth defects. If we ingest particles of materials that emit dangerous radiation, those particles remain inside us, continually subjecting us to low doses of radiation. That may seem less dangerous than a single blast of high-energy gamma rays, but damage from radiation is cumulative. Long exposure to low doses can result in the same damage as short exposure to a high dose. We don't want our food to contain particles, however small, of radioactive matter. Nor do we want to be exposed to high (or repetitive low) doses of high-energy radiation. The radiation technology used in food preservation avoids both of those problems. First, food never touches the irradiating source. Instead, food passes through an area that is 'illuminated' by the radiation of choice. The type of radiation chosen depends on the foods being treated.

Gamma radiation is, obviously, the most powerful. Depending on the source, it can penetrate foods of different thicknesses. Cobalt-60 is the strongest source of gamma rays, and can penetrate further into foods than other isotopes. Caesium-137 is preferred for foods that aren't very thick because it doesn't need to be replaced as often as Cobalt-60 (meaning that Caesium-137 is a less expensive alternative to Cobalt-60). For safety, heavy lead shielding separates food workers from either source of radiation.

Electron beams do not require a radioactive isotope. They can be used to irradiate food, but they consume a lot of power, and cannot penetrate very far into the targeted food unless converted into X-rays, which require still more electricity and heavy shielding similar to that used in gamma-ray processing.

A less-threatening form of irradiation is ultraviolet light, which is an ideal process of preservation for those foods that are able to be pumped past a very bright source of this light. Think of it as an extreme tanning bed. New York City's water is famously pleasant-tasting because it substitutes a blast of ultraviolet light for the unpleasant chlorine used in most other cities. Fruit juices and dairy products are commonly treated this way, as this method avoids changes to flavour that can result from the heat of pasteurization.

The good news for consumers is that when ionizing radiation passes through food it kills pathogens without changing the food itself – and it leaves no trace of radiation within the food. Since we are not exposed either to radiation or radioactive particles, we are not subject to any bad effects from the resulting preserved food.

High Pressure Processing

High-pressure processing (HPP, also known as bridgmanization or pascalization) is one of our newest food-preservation technologies. Foods are sealed in flexible containers, such as heavy plastic bags, submersed in a tank filled with water and then subjected to extremely high pressure. This kills any bacteria living in the food. It does not, however, kill all bacterial spores. Consequently, the technique is used for relatively acidic foods, such as fruit, salad dressings and yoghurt, that discourage spore germination.

Guacamole preserved with high-pressure processing. Note the label that boasts '100% Fresh Ingredients' and 'No Preservatives'.

In recent years, refrigerated sections of grocery stores in the U.S. have carried plastic pouches of bridgmanized guacamole that stay fresh for weeks.

Foods preserved by HPP are not heated and require no additional salt, so their flavours are unaffected. They are not frozen, so their textures are unchanged. They also require no preservatives. While the process is not ideal for all foods, those that can undergo it are kept in a 'fresher' condition than those that use any other preservation technique.

Hurdle Technology

Hurdle technology combines multiple preservation techniques, often in a sequence that systematically removes a series of obstacles to safe storage. A food may be fermented and then dried, like black tea and black pepper. It may be dried, reconstituted and then fermented, like leavened bread products, created from grains that are dried, ground, rehydrated and finally fermented by yeasts. Some grains are fermented, but not baked into breads. They are prepared as a form of porridge. Kenyans pound an assortment of mixed grains (maize, millet and/or sorghum) to make *uchuru*, a starchy liquid that they pour into gourds and leave in the sun to ferment.

Himalayan *gundrik* is a form of preserved vegetables, mainly comprising cabbages, mustard greens and radish greens. They are partly dried in the sun, then fermented without salt and completely dried. Radish roots, however, are first fermented, then chopped and dried, to make *sinki*.

Many foods are first salted and fermented, and then canned or bottled – think of sauerkraut, or all of the soya products used in Asian cookery. Grain can be malted, dried, sprouted, toasted, rehydrated, fermented to produce alcohol, partially dehydrated (distilled) and aged in wood, then bottled to prevent evaporation of what has become whisky. Pascalized foods can be acidified to prevent the germination of surviving bacterial spores. Sausages may be salted, fermented, smoked and dried. 'Fresh' (neither fermented nor dried) sausages are salted then frozen.

FOUR
Major Ingredients

S ometimes we're merely oblivious to the presence of preservatives and stabilizers that make our food seem fresh,
while reaching into our refrigerators and freezers seems just
as natural as plucking fruit from a tree would have been for our
ancestors. However, many foods are not perceived as 'preserved'
simply because they have been part of our diets for so long. Ham is
no longer seen as preserved pork, for example: it's just ham.

Meat

Bacon, hams and sausages use salt, smoke and sometimes sugar
to prevent them from going the way of all flesh – and creating
flavours and textures never found in nature. Meat is among the
most perishable of foodstuffs, yet it made up a substantial part of
the hunter-gatherers' diets. Proteins and moisture in meat make
it very appealing to all sorts of microorganisms (and macroorgan-
isms; early humans competed with all sorts of other scavengers).
Even without freeloading creatures, enzymes in the meat itself
begin the process of decomposition shortly after the animal's
demise. A little decomposition is not dangerous. When we age
beef, we are allowing those enzymes to partly digest it, although
we prefer to think of this process as 'tenderizing'. In the past,
people actually preferred the taste of slightly rotten meats, less
threateningly characterized as 'high' or 'well-hung'. Game was

**To Keepe Venison Fresh
a Long Time (1588)**

Presse out the blood cleane, and put it into an earthen
pot, and fill it with clarified Honey two fingers aboue
the fleshe, and binde a Leather close about the mouth
that no ayre enter.[1]

left to hang for periods of time that would seem disgusting to
modern palates.

Long before our ancestors learned about bacteria, they discovered that keeping meats away from air slowed the rate of
decomposition. While they did not have canning facilities, certain other techniques were available to them, as the recipes given
here show.

By the nineteenth century, some modern squeamishness had
begun to change our tastes. *The Cook's Own Book, and Housekeeper's
Register* (1832) suggested:

> Tainted meat may be restored by washing in cold water,
> afterwards in strong chamomile tea, after which it may
> be sprinkled with salt and used the following day, first
> washing it in cold water. Roughly pounded charcoal
> rubbed all over the meat also restores it when tainted.
> In Scotland meat is frequently kept a fortnight smoth-
> ered in oatmeal, and carefully wiped every day; and if it
> should be a little tainted, it is soaked some hours before
> it is used, in oatmeal and water.[2]

Despite such questionable recommendations, the earliest reliable
methods for keeping meats beyond their natural expiration dates
were certainly drying, smoking and – where available – salting. To

some extent, we are still using these techniques, albeit with a bit more understanding of the underlying principles.

Our pantry (or pocket) might hold a variety of dried and cured meats, including all sorts of hunter's sausages: German *Jagdwurst* and *Landjäger*; Italian *cacciatore* and *cacciatorini*; Anatolian *pasturma* and other air-dried meats from all over the former Ottoman Empire; and even American Slim Jims. Brazilian *carne seca* and Mexican *carneseca* are strips of air-dried beef used in cooking. Thin slices of beef or pork in a crust of ground chillies become Mexican air-dried *cecinas*. Milder Spanish *cecina* might even be made from goat, hare, horse or rabbit meat.

Indonesians make several similar dessicated meats called *dendeng*. Sweet *dendeng sapi* is beef cured with coconut, while *dendeng rusa* is made from venison. Their *bakkwa* is like *dendeng*, but can be made from sliced chicken, beef or pork, and may be spicy or mild. The sweet and salty Vietnamese dehydrated *rousong* is also popular among the Chinese, Malaysians, Filipinos and Taiwanese. It is made by slowly cooking pork in a sugary soy sauce until it falls apart into shreds – something like an Asian version of pulled pork, or a *ropa vieja* – and then drying it. Observant Muslims substitute beef for pork in Indonesia's *abon*, or with beef or chicken in Malaysian *serunding*.

Many variations of jerky are made around the world, tinkering with ingredients and flavours to suit local tastes. A South African version, called *biltong*, utilizes game or farmed ostrich. Replacing some of the salt, vinegar provides the acidity needed to discourage bacteria. Ethiopian *qwant'a* adds a spicier touch with lots of black pepper and *berberé*, a North African chilli paste composed of various herbs and spices. Algerians and Moroccans dry strips of marinated meat – beef, camel, goat or lamb – in the sun to make *gueddid*. Oddly enough, it is preserved by several strains of the lactic-acid-producing bacterium *Enterococcus faecium* from the animals' intestines. The Chinese version of *bakkwa* (*rougan*) is beef, mutton or pork, marinated in a mixture of five-spice powder,

Sliced *biltong,* a South African version of jerky. It is usually seasoned with several spices (cloves, coriander and pepper) and preserved with salt-petre and vinegar.

salt, soy sauce and sugar, and then dried. Italian charcuterie also includes a hot and spicy jerky that is called *coppiette*. Pork is the most common type, although it was formerly made from donkey or horse. Today's commercial jerky is mostly marinated, smoked and dosed with sodium nitrite. It is vacuum-packed in plastic, and this packaging method allows for one-handed consumption, which makes it easy to consume while driving, for example, explaining its omnipresence at truck stops in the U.S.

Ham and sausage production has, historically, been the most significant consumer of salt (at least for preserving meats). We know from surviving Sumerian clay tablets of 1600 BCE that Mesopotamians salted meats, and that ancient Egyptian wall paintings showed black puddings being made from the blood of sacrificial cattle. However, *The Odyssey* contains the earliest literary accounts of sausages:

> . . . here are goat stomachs ready on the fire
> to stuff with blood and fat, good supper pudding,
> The man who wins this gallant bout

Basic Sausage

This is the simplest possible recipe; it provides the starting point for any kind of sausage. You need only decide on kind of protein, seasoning, texture, size, casing or no casing, smoking or not, fresh or dried, fermented or not – there are infinite variations!

Makes 5 pounds (2.25 kg)

4 lb (1.8 kg) meat, fish or poultry
1 lb (450 g) firm fat (pork or beef), nearly frozen
1 oz (30 g) sea (kosher) salt
6 oz (180 ml) ice water
herbs or spices of your choice
casings, if desired, soaked and well rinsed

Cut the meat and fat into 25-mm (1-inch) cubes, discarding any bits of gristle or bone. Mix the meat with the salt and desired seasoning in a non-reactive bowl; cover and chill in refrigerator for at least four hours or overnight. Chill grinder at the same time. Grind or chop the meat to desired texture. Add ice water. Mix ground mixture until it becomes sticky. Stuff sausage into casings, or form into patties. Refrigerate the fresh sausage until ready to cook. Otherwise, wrap tightly, in pre-portioned packages of cling film, and freeze – or continue with additional processes (like drying, smoking or curing, which may require the use of curing agents and/or preservatives).[3]

may step up here and take the one he likes. (Book 18,
lines 16–19)

. . . rolling from side to side
as a cook turns a sausage, big with blood
and fat, at a scorching blaze, without a pause,
to broil it quick . . . (Book 20, lines 24–7)

Bacon can be smoked or not, air-dried or not, and it can be
made of various portions of the pig. American bacon ('the cured
belly of a swine carcass', according to the USDA) and Italian *pancetta* are usually made from belly or side meat. It is known as
'streaky bacon' in the UK. Bacons from the top of the pig have
practically no lean meat, and are known as 'fatback' or 'salt pork'.
Generally unsmoked, they provide the unctuous and flavourful
lardons of French cooking. Italian *lardo* and Eastern European *salo*
are forms of cured and seasoned pork fat that are consumed raw,
rather than as ingredients in cooking. *Salos* vary geographically:
they are generally unsmoked in the northern parts of Ukraine,
but smoked further south. Similar *salos* are found in most Slavic
countries; while their names and seasonings change, they are all

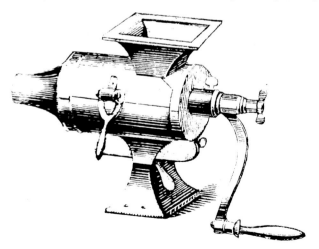

Unusual 19th-
century sausage
grinder.

Davies' Bacon poster,
c. 1900.

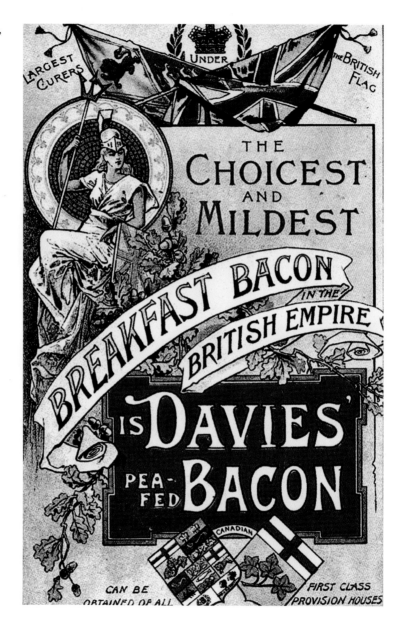

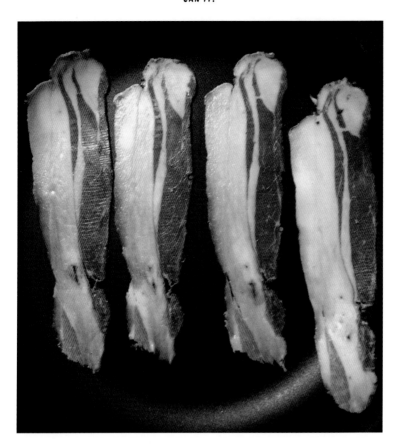

Bacon made from the belly of a mangalitza pig.

raw salt-cured pig fat. Canadian bacon has very little fat; it is made from boneless loin. Green bacon is British unsmoked belly or sidemeat, while Italian *guanciale* is air-cured, but unsmoked, jowl bacon. Hungarian *kolozsvári szalonna* is smoked, but also rubbed with garlic. In Japan *bekon* is cured, smoked and pre-cooked; it has a consistency similar to slices of American country ham. For those who do not eat pork, bacon substitutes are sometimes made from other meats, such as turkey or beef, and even from soya protein for vegetarians.

Bacon is generally cured either in brine or in a salty crust. Either way, the active ingredients are salt and some form of nitrite,

Lardo – salted, cured and spiced pork fat – traditionally made in the vicinity of Cararra, Italy.

though it may also include sugars, spices and other ingredients, such as Graham's salt (sodium polyphosphate, a fat stabilizer). American and British bacons are smoked as a slab, while Italian *pancetta* is rolled tightly and aged in the air; the latter is milder-tasting, and is distinguished by some of the fermented flavours found in *prosciutto*.

Guanciale, a cured but unsmoked Italian bacon made from the jowls of pigs.

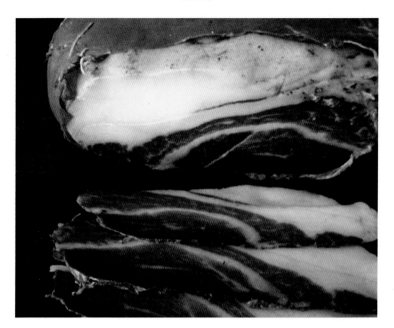

Ham may be everyone's second favourite salted meat (obviously, bacon is first). Hams are cured virtually everywhere that pigs are raised – which is everywhere except places that are too dry or too cold. To the best of my knowledge, no swine are farmed in Antarctica, and few, if any, in the arid Middle East. Varieties of salt-cured pork range from the delicately brined *petit salé* of France to the nearly rock-hard country hams of Virginia. The deep umami flavour of China's *Jinhua* ham is a result of fermentation by moulds and yeasts. Added to traditional Chinese dishes, like Buddha Jumps over the Wall, it can reputedly tempt even the most vigilant vegetarians to abandon their principles. Salt-cured hams can be smoked, like Germany's *Schwarzwälder Schinken* and England's York ham, or they can be air-cured, without smoke, like Spain's *jamón ibérico* and Italy's *prosciutto di Parma*. Prosciutto is an unsmoked dry-cured ham, like American country hams (though some country hams are smoked). *Prosciutto crudo*, like the Spanish *jamón*, is uncooked and served raw in paper-thin slices. Country

Early 20th-century label. Note the 'Fidelity' brand – a suggestion of honesty and purity in a time when the public was newly concerned with food safety issues.

Aerial view of the Hormel plant, postcard, *c.* 1960.

hams are hard as a rock; they can last, unrefrigerated, for years, but need to be soaked for days before being roasted. Whether they are as sweet as *culatello*, as fiery as *capicola* or as smoky as *Speck*, they remain quintessentially *ham*.

Wet-cured hams are just that: they are soaked in, or injected with, brine. Either way, the goal is the same. Salt travels through the meat, pulling water osmotically from the meat's cells. This concentrates protein molecules that are too big to be drawn through cell membranes, thereby firming the flesh. In the process, amino acids and peptides interact (sometimes with other ingredients in the salt or brine), forming new compounds that create the distinctive 'ham' taste and aroma. In addition to salt, brines might contain spices, molasses and/or beer. The brine for English Suffolk ham, for example, uses stout.

Hormel's 'Flavor-sealed Hams' first appeared in cans – oddly shaped things that only hinted at their gelatine-coated contents – in 1926. Hams are not the only meats to wear full metal jackets. Spam first found its way into an iconic blue Hormel can in 1937. Originally made of ham and pork shoulder meat, and sugar – united by salt and modified potato starch, and preserved by sodium nitrite – Spam now comes in over a dozen other flavours, some formulated for particular markets, such as the Asian market.

Like ham, delicatessen meats – the 'cold cuts' destined to fill sandwiches – are invariably preserved. That obviously includes all the various sausages, from bologna to salami to mysterious blocks of 'luncheon loaf', but also corned beef and pastrami that are brined (or dry-cured, crusted with grains – 'corn' – of salt and spices) and may be partially dried or smoked as well. Montreal's famous 'smoked meat' is not just a type of pastrami, it is the proto-typical pastrami of our dreams – old-fashioned, made-on-the-spot, savoury bliss that is served without fanfare to neighbours and travelling foodies alike.

The French have their *rillettes* – meats, poultry, game or fish that are slowly cooked, shredded, then packed in a crock to age under a protective layer of solidified fat – and *confits*: duck, rabbit

Hickory-smoked
Spam.

or goose, slowly simmered in the fat that will cover it. Like confit, Moroccans poach *gueddid* (dried beef) in oil and animal fat to make *khlea*. It is packed into large jars, with all the voids carefully filled with the cooking liquid, and stored for up to two years.

The empty spaces around pâtés and terrines are often filled with firm aspic to protect the meat while its seasonings slowly meld with the meat. Guillaume Tirel offered some instructions (that probably wouldn't be welcome in today's kitchens) for making meat-preserving gelatine given opposite.

Rillettes, confits, pâtés and terrines – as well as jellied sausages, like headcheese and souse, and the Flemish dish *potjevleesch* – are variations on the theme of 'potted meats'. Sometimes, these preserved 'mystery meats' were intended to mimic the flesh of more expensive or preferred creatures.

Modern mass-produced potted meats come in cans. Canned meats have had varying degrees of popularity over the decades. Spam and Underwood Deviled Ham are obvious examples. Several companies (Armour, Hormel, Libby's) make similar canned meat products that feature 'mechanically separated' chicken

Coppa calabrese, a spicy *capocollo* made with plenty of red pepper – sometimes seen as 'hot capicollo' in the U.S.

Coppa piacentina, a style of cured pork made in Piacenza. The name is protected, in Italy, by the Consorzio dei Salumi Tipici Piacentini – although this particular *coppa* was made in Orange County, New York.

Jelly of Slimy Fish, and of Meat
(14th century)

Cook it in wine, verjuice and vinegar. Some add a bit of water. Take ginger, cassia, cloves, grains of paradise and long pepper, steep in your broth, strain through cheesecloth, and boil with your meat. Take bay leaves, spike lavender, galingale and mace, tie in your cheesecloth (without washing it) with the dregs of the other spices, and boil with your meat. Cover it while it is on the fire, but when it is off the fire, skim it until it is set out.

When it is cooked, [strain] your broth into a clean wooden dish until it is settled. Put your meat on a white cloth. If it is fish, peel and clean it, and throw your peelings in the broth until it is strained the last time. Make sure your broth is clear and clean.

Now set your meat out in bowls. Put your broth back on the fire in a clear and clean dish, boil it, and while it is boiling throw it on your meat. Sprinkle cassia flowers and mace over the plates or bowls where you put your meat and broth, and put your plates in a cold place to set. If you wish to make jelly, you do not need to sleep. If your broth is not very clean and clear, strain it through two or three layers of white cloth. On your meat, if it is fish, put crayfish tails and feet, and cooked loach.[4]

> ## Potted Beef as Venison (1847)
>
> Choose a piece of lean beef from the buttock, or other part that has no bone in it; rub it all over with saltpeter, and let it lie twelve hours, then salt it thoroughly with bay salt and common salt in equal parts, well blended. Place it in a pot that will only just contain it; let it be completely covered with water, and remain thus four days; then wipe it well with a cloth, and rub it with pepper beaten to a powder; lay it into a pot without any liquor; put over it a crust of brown flour, and let it bake like large loaves six or seven hours; then take it out, and when it is cool enough pick out all the strings and skins, and beat it in a stone mortar finely. The seasoning must be mace, cloves, and nutmeg reduced to a fine powder; and add a little melted butter in which flour has been absorbed; put it down in pots as closely as you can, and pour clarified butter over it.[5]

(and other meats) – also known by the less appetizing term 'pink slime' – along with offal that has been ground into unrecognizability. Their preservatives (sodium erythorbate and sodium nitrite) actually sound less frightening than the main ingredients. Treet (a Spam competitor made of chicken and pork), Vienna Sausages (cocktail wieners), Deviled Ham, Dinty Moore Beef Stew and several brands of chilli still sit on shop shelves, although I'm not sure Underwood Deviled Tongue does (even if you may, as it was once advertised, 'Eat it without a guilty conscience.')

As frightening as some of these preserved meats might appear, consider them against the fare of sea-goers of the past.

Potted meat: seasoned, mechanically separated beef tripe and chicken.

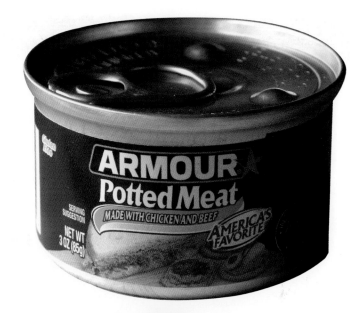

Bresaolina di cervo affumicata, air-dried and smoked venison.

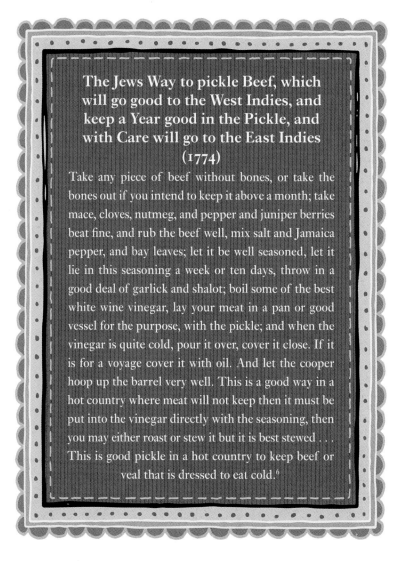

The Jews Way to pickle Beef, which will go good to the West Indies, and keep a Year good in the Pickle, and with Care will go to the East Indies (1774)

Take any piece of beef without bones, or take the bones out if you intend to keep it above a month; take mace, cloves, nutmeg, and pepper and juniper berries beat fine, and rub the beef well, mix salt and Jamaica pepper, and bay leaves; let it be well seasoned, let it lie in this seasoning a week or ten days, throw in a good deal of garlick and shalot; boil some of the best white wine vinegar, lay your meat in a pan or good vessel for the purpose, with the pickle; and when the vinegar is quite cold, pour it over, cover it close. If it is for a voyage cover it with oil. And let the cooper hoop up the barrel very well. This is a good way in a hot country where meat will not keep then it must be put into the vinegar directly with the seasoning, then you may either roast or stew it but it is best stewed . . . This is good pickle in a hot country to keep beef or veal that is dressed to eat cold.[6]

Shipboard tales and travellers journeys frequently mention – in a groaning, resigned kind of way – the inevitable, eternal, indestructible salted meat that was the staple protein for officers, crew, and passengers alike. This 'salt horse' . . .

First World War magazine advertisement for Underwood's Deviled Tongue, 1918.

UNDERWOOD
Deviled Tongue

"Eat it Without a Guilty Conscience"

[All Rights Reserved]

CONSERVATION today is the world's crying need. In order to save lives, we are saving not only coal, sugar, wheat, fats—but also many *essential forms of meats.*

Every American housewife can serve Underwood Deviled Tongue with a clear conscience, knowing that she is thereby helping to save those "essential" meats for our soldiers and Allies overseas.

And it will be a pleasure instead of a hardship. Underwood Deviled Tongue has a fresh, appetizing flavor, the kind of flavor that has made Underwood Deviled Ham famous.

Delicious tongue, cooked *en casserole* to keep in all its choice delicacy, then chopped fine and mixed with the famous Underwood Deviled Dressing of mild spices—that's what it is! Just taste it—in omelets, croquettes, sandwiches—just as you use Underwood Deviled Ham.

"GOOD TASTES FOR GOOD TIMES" is a book of 66 famous little Red Devil Recipes—new, unusual dishes for every meal. Free. Write us for it. And order a can of Underwood Deviled Tongue from your grocer today—two sizes, 20c and 35c. If your grocer has not yet received a supply, send us his name and address and 20c, and we will send you an economical can to try.

Everybody must eat *some* meat, but everybody can help save the "essential meats" by getting the Underwood Deviled Tongue habit.

WM. UNDERWOOD CO.
52 Fulton Street Boston Mass.

DEVILED TONGUE HASH

MIX with Underwood Deviled Tongue three times its bulk of mashed or chopped potato. Season with salt and moisten with soup stock or water. Melt a tablespoonful of butter in a frying pan, put in the hash, and cook slowly and evenly till a brown crust is formed on the bottom. Loosen from the pan with a knife and fold like an omelet. Serve hot.

"TASTE THE TASTE"

"BRANDED WITH THE DEVIL BUT FIT FOR THE GODS"

Mincemeat (1861)

Ingredients. – 2 lbs. of raisins, 3 lbs. of currants, 1-½ lb. of lean beef, 3 lbs. of beef suet, 2 lbs. of moist sugar, 2 oz. of citron, 2 oz. of candied lemon-peel, 2 oz. of candied orange-peel, 1 small nutmeg, 1 pottle of apples, the rind of 2 lemons, the juice of 1½ pint of brandy.

Mode. – Stone and cut the raisins once or twice across, but do not chop them; wash, dry, and pick the currants free from stalks and grit, and mince the beef and suet, taking care that the latter is chopped very fine; slice the citron and candied peel, grate the nutmeg, and pare, core, and mince the apples; mince the lemon-peel, strain the juice, and when all the ingredients are thus prepared, mix them well together, adding the brandy when the other things are well blended; press the whole into a jar, carefully exclude the air, and the mince meat will be ready for use in a fortnight.[7]

[was] so old and so tough and so salty that the day's ration was often towed behind the ship on a long rope before being returned to the galley – such treatment apparently making it marginally more cookable and palatable.[8]

Today, if we even think of mincemeat, it is just a jar in the supermarket – a brownish mass of some unknown material that barely contains meat, other than beef suet. In fact, the pie filling has a long history that blurs the boundary between modern notions

Advertisement for Atmore's products, *c*. 1885.

87

of sweet and savoury. It is practically medieval, which is, perhaps, why we still serve it during cold-weather holidays. Holidays are a time when we gather family together and consume foods that have barely changed over generations, or even centuries.

The recipe given here comes from the venerable Mrs Beeton, and is comparatively modern for mincemeat. Don't be puzzled by the measurement 'pottle' – this means a half-gallon (1.9 litres).

Mince pies, today, are either loved or hated (except by those who have no idea what they are). Apparently, the situation wasn't much different 150 years ago:

> Perhaps, after all, the use of apples chopped fine and mixed with meat, as in mince pies, is as objectionable as any. These mince pies, when made in the best manner, are bad enough; but when made up not only with lean meat, but with the addition of suet, spices, raw and dried fruits, wine, brandy, &c., and put into the usual forms of pastry, they become – as Dr Paris says of pastry alone – an abomination.[9]

Fish

Fish make up the second part of the three primary proteins in our larders (with dairy making the third). In our refrigerators, sliced lox and plastic tubs of shucked oysters await us. In the freezer section, we find frozen fillets from fresh and salt waters, ready-made crab cakes, lobster tails from tropical seas, bags of prawns of all sizes (cooked or raw), cleaned bodies and tentacles of squid, and giant legs of king crabs from the Bering Sea. Fish, and other seafood, are also good candidates for preserving: they are highly perishable, rich in nutrients (proteins and fats), and easily acquired in much greater quantities than can be immediately consumed. The earliest preservation method was drying, and it is still used today. Salting accelerates drying, and is especially important where humidity prevents fast-enough dehydration. In regions that lack salt, or have insufficiently arid conditions, smoking and pickling have long been used to aid in the preserving process.

Stockfish may once have been the staple protein of the masses but today our staple preserved fish comes in cans or plastic pouches. Rather than cod, tuna is the catch of the day. Canned tuna has probably provided more sandwich fillings, salad plates and casseroles than any other modern seafood. Occasionally, in an old-school Italian shop, we will see barrels of entire dried *baccalà* but, more often, we're lucky to find even little wooden boxes of salt cod.

The North Atlantic is a cold and unforgiving place, yet it teems with fish. Historically, cod and herring have been the most important preserved fish – at least in countries that surround the Atlantic Ocean. Seagoing Vikings may have been the first to exploit the vast offshore fishery:

> What did these Norsemen eat on the five expeditions to America between 985 and 1011 that have been recorded in the Icelandic sagas? They were able to travel to all those distant, barren shores because they had learned to preserve codfish by hanging it in the frosty winter air until it lost four-fifths of its weight . . . in the ninth century, Norsemen had already established plants for processing dried cod in Iceland and Norway and were trading the surplus in northern Europe.[10]

Viking dried cod was a valuable commodity, but it did not keep as well as the Basques' salt cod. Basque traders were able to expand the cod market much further, well into the Mediterranean, where no cod ever swam, but where the inhabitants had relished other salted foods for millennia. Salt cod became a fixture of European cuisine that would last for centuries. *Le Ménagier de Paris* made these suggestions at the end of the fourteenth century:

Salt cod for sale at a Nice market.

When it is taken in the far seas and it is desired to keep it for ten or twelve years, it is gutted and its head removed and it is dried in the air and sun and in no wise by a fire, or smoked; and when this is done it is called stockfish. And when it hath been kept a long time and it is desired to eat it, it behoves to beat it with a wooden hammer for a full hour, and then set it to soak in warm water for a full two hours or more, then cook and scour it very well like beef; then eat it with mustard or soaked in butter. And if any remain in the evening, let it be fried in small pieces like shreds and spice powder thereon.[11]

Stockfish were carried to the New World, until New Englanders learned about the huge shoals of cod on the Grand Banks which Basque fishermen had kept secret for six centuries. The strongly mercantile Yankees never replaced the Basques in the Mediterranean, but they turned salt cod into a commodity that could be used in a triangular system of trade that involved African slaves and Caribbean sugar, molasses and rum. One preserved food begot another, with human misery providing the medium of exchange.

Haddock, like cod, is a lean white-fleshed fish, often eaten fresh or frozen. Haddock is preserved by drying or smoking, not salted in the manner of cod. 'Arbroath smokie' is one name for Scottish smoked haddock, but much more familiarly:

> Finnan haddie, a haddock soaked in brine and then smoked over peat and sawdust, was originally called Findon haddocks because it was made in the Scottish North Sea town of Findon, near Aberdeen. It was not commercialized until the mid-eighteenth century, though it may have been a household product for a long time before that.[12]

Cod are certainly not the only dried fish. Northern India's misnamed 'Bombay duck' is a variety of lizardfish (*Harpadon nehereus*). While they can be eaten fresh, they are more often dried and salted, becoming extremely 'fragrant' – to put it delicately – and used as an umami-laden condiment with curries.

Atlantic and Pacific salmons are anadromous: that is, they are born in fresh water, but migrate to salt water, where they put on

Preserving the huge annual runs of salmon by drying and smoking had been a priority of native peoples in the Pacific Northwest for centuries; canning in Alaska began in 1878. The earliest cans were painted red, so most labels continued that tradition.

Drying salt cod, Kirkjusandur, Iceland, late 19th century.

most of their weight, then return to the spot where they hatched in order to spawn. Pacific species die after spawning, but Atlantic salmon can return to the sea, and even spawn again. The migratory habits of salmonids – returning each year in vast numbers to relatively small rivers – have made them ideal fish for preserving, since fishermen can acquire vast quantities of these fish in a short space of time. Salmon have long been cured, dried and/or smoked. 'Lox' – a word that can trace its ancestry all the way back to the Indo-European *laks* – refers to salmon that has been filleted before being brined. It may, or may not, be smoked afterwards. Scottish, Nordic and Nova Scotia ('Nova') lox are cold-smoked, while gravlax is only cured. The name is derived from the process by which the fillets were originally buried and left to cure in both a sweet and salty rub of dill, salt and sometimes sugar and juniper berries. Salmon contain a lot of fat, so they don't dry well enough for truly long-term storage, although native peoples from the Pacific Northwest have lived on air-dried salmon for centuries. These rich fish freeze well.

The closely related trout are largely freshwater species, though brook, brown and rainbow trout will occasionally migrate to the sea. Most trout are too small or too difficult to catch in large quantities to justify commercial preservation (although Norwegians salt and ferment them to make *rakfisk*, which they serve raw, accompanied by sour cream and onions). One somewhat more familiar exception to this is farm-raised rainbow trout. Trout are typically available frozen or smoked.

Atlantic herring are rich in fat, which made them valuable before modern sedentary lifestyles made obesity a concern. Pacific herring are nearly identical and, despite their name, are not limited to the Pacific and Indian Oceans; they often appear on Mediterranean menus. Unfortunately, herring's fats easily become rancid, so they don't lend themselves to drying and salting. Herring are generally pickled or smoked (the 'red herrings' so beloved of mystery writers are highly odoriferous smoked fish, alleged to have been dragged along, often by the Master of Hounds, creating a false trail to distract the hounds during fox hunts, hence their meaning: a purposely misleading clue).

> Red herring, a famous export from the East Anglia region of England along the North Sea, is soaked in a brine of salt and saltpeter and then smoked over oak and turf. The discovery of red herring was described by a native East Anglian, Thomas Nash, in 1567. He claimed that it came about when a Yarmouth fisherman with an unusually large catch hung the surplus herring on a rafter, and by chance the room had an unusually smoky fire.[13]

Like salmon, herring are anadromous. Unlike salmon, they spawn in the spring, and huge numbers can be scooped out of shallow streams with simple hand nets. If the herring are caught before spawning, when their fat content is highest, they are known as shmaltz herring, after the Yiddish word for fat. Herring are often pickled after being salted; the pickling ingredients vary, but generally include sugar, vinegar and a mix of spices.

Seventeenth-century Dutch herring *busses* – precursors of today's factory ships – salted and barrelled the highly perishable fish at sea. The Dutch dominated the industry until the mid-nineteenth century, when herring numbers declined in the North Sea and Norwegian and Scottish fleets were better able to harvest the schools of North Atlantic herring. Eventually, over-fishing took its toll on these once immense fisheries. In 1928, William Butler Yeats described 'mackerel-crowded seas' in 'Sailing to Byzantium', his elegy to what 'is past, or passing', but he had already lamented, in 1896, 'The herring are not in the tides as they were of old.'[14]

Pickled herrings, such as Germany's *Bismarckhering*, have been a mainstay of northern Europe – at least since railways made quick transportation of *Rollmopse* to interior regions possible. Refrigerated jars of pickled herring are not just a European phenomenon; the Japanese version features reconstituted dried salted herring, marinated in various Japanese rice vinegars, sake, shoyu and perhaps a little wasabi.

Atlantic mackerel and related Pacific mackerel are forage fish often found in coastal waters. Because of their high oil content, they are generally preserved either by freezing or pickling.

Today we think of sushi as the *ne plus ultra* of freshness and elegant refinement in seafood 'cookery', but it originated as long ago as the second century BCE as a way to use leftover salted fish – like herring – as lunches for labourers. It wasn't until the mid-nineteenth century that supremely fresh bits of fish began to appear atop rice seasoned with sweetened vinegar. Today's sushi bars, especially in the U.S., have begun to make special sushi rolls using smoked salmon, and even, in some extremely non-traditional instances, cream cheese. These are called Philadelphia (or Philly) rolls.

Westerners, especially those acquainted with Jewish delis, or 'appetizing stores', are more familiar with other salted fish: lox (smoked salmon), gravlax, sable (smoked black cod), chubs (brined and smoked whitefish that has been dyed yellow), kippers (smoked herring) and delicately cold-smoked sturgeon.

Unlike many Chinese sauces, which are named for the foods they accompany rather than their ingredients, oyster sauce is actually made from oysters.

Pilchards and sardines – generic names for small herring – are more frequently seen in their canned form than fresh, and they are only occasionally frozen. In the original French canning method, beheaded and eviscerated sardines were first fried, then packed (yes, like sardines) in tins, along with olive oil. Most canned sardines today are packed raw, but are then cooked in the can during processing. Packing liquids can be mustard, oil, tomato sauce or plain water.

The Engraulidae family consists of 144 species of anchovy – oily fish that are related to herrings. Anchovies are usually cured in brine, which gives them a strong taste that is slightly bitter, similar to capers, with which they are sometimes packed. They come packed in small tins, or as tubes of paste. They can be eaten on their own, but their intense flavour often serves as an ingredient in other foods, such as a topping for Neapolitan pizza or Provençal *pissaladière*, or to add a blast of salty umami to sauces. The ancient Romans fermented anchovies into *garum*, a salty fish sauce used in most of their dishes (*garum* was to Rome what soy sauce is to China). The Romans made several variations of the sauce: *meligarum*, sweetened with honey; *oenogarum*, mixed with wine; and *oxygarum*, tart with vinegar. *Colatura di alici*, an anchovy-based fish sauce still made from Naples to the Amalfi Coast, is a direct descendant of *garum*. Fermented anchovies, combined with a blend of locally favoured spices (coriander, cumin, fennel and mustard), produce *mahyawa*, a bottled fish sauce from the Persian Gulf. Burmese *ngan bya yay*, Indonesian *ketjap-ikan*, Thai *nam pla* and Vietnamese *nước mâm* – generally made with anchovies

95

> ## To Pickle or Bake Mackrel, to Keep all the Year (1774)
>
> Gut them, cut off their heads, cut them open, dry them very well with a clean cloth, take a pan which they will lie cleverly in, lay a few bay-leaves at the bottom, rub the bone with a little bay-salt beat fine, take a little beaten mace, a few cloves beat fine, black and white pepper beat fine; mix a little salt, rub them inside and out with the spice, lay them in a pan, and between every lay of mackrel put a few bay-leaves; then cover them with vinegar, tie them down close with brown paper, put them in a slow oven: they will take a good while doing; when they are enough, uncover them, let them stand till cold; then pour away all that vinegar, and put as much good vinegar as will cover them, and put in an onion stuck with cloves. Send them to the oven again, let them stand two hours in a very slow oven, and they will keep all the year; but you must not put in your hands to take out the mackrel, if you can avoid it, but take a slice to take them out with.[15]

– are probably very close to *garum*. Thai 'Squid Brand' *nam pla* is a misnomer; it contains no squid, just anchovies and salt. *Pla ra*, a variation on Thai *nam pla*, substitutes snakehead murrel – a fresh-water species – for traditional anchovies. It is fermented, in salt and rice bran, for up to one year. *Patis* and *bagoong terong*, from the Philippines, are similar, but are not made in quite the same manner. They are by-products made when the excess liquid is drained from the fermented fish paste *bagoong*. Conversely, ancient Romans also saved the settled solids from of their *garum* vats. They called it *allec*. Special *allecs* were made, as primary products, from oysters, sea urchins and the livers of mullets.

Much like *nam pla*, the Japanese fish sauce *shottsuru* is a thin salty liquid. It is made from *hatahata*, a local species of sandfish (*Arctoscopus japonicus*). Japan also has similar sauces made from other fishes: *ishiru*, from sardines and squid; and *kanago shoyu*, from sand lances (Ammodytidae spp.). The name of the latter sauce indicates that it is used like soy sauce, providing a burst of salt and umami. Korean *kanari* is also brewed from fermented sand lances, while their *saewoojeot* is made from shrimp.

Colombo cure is pickled fish from the west coast of India. Seer fish (a type of Spanish or king mackerel) are fermented with salt and tamarind, which provide additional acidity to preserve the fish. Malaysian *budu* also uses tamarind, plus palm sugar to promote Maillard browning. *Budu* is now available, in Malaysia, as a dehydrated seasoning powder.

An ordinary sardine tin, serving up umami, calories and protein in each fishy morsel.

Tuna has been dried and salted, in Spain, for centuries. This *mojama*, like salt cod, is preferred over fresh fish. The traditional salting method is based on a much older recipe – used to produce the *musama* that the Moors made in Spain before they were expelled in the fifteenth century. In Japan, skipjack tuna is fermented with mould (*Aspergillus glaucus*), smoked, shaved into paper-thin strips and dried. The resulting *katsuobushi* can be eaten directly as a garnish, for example on iced tofu. More frequently, it – or dried bonito – is combined with *kombu* (dried kelp) to make the broth called *dashi*. For Japanese cooks, *dashi* is as fundamental in cooking as stock is for the French.

Spanish tuna in olive oil. Note that the box indicates that the enclosed can has a pull tab: no old-fashioned can-opener required.

Indonesian skipjack tuna are processed in an unusual way. The fish are scaled and eviscerated, then split lengthwise, leaving the head and tail portions intact. They are stretched over a bamboo rack, rubbed with a mixture of salt and baking soda (sodium bicarbonate), and smoked for up to four hours. Prepared in this way, they will keep, even in tropical conditions, for a month or so.

Botargo is the firm, dried roe sacs of various types of fish, used throughout the Mediterranean region as a condiment when grated or as an appetizer when thinly sliced. It is commonly made from flathead mullet in Greece, Sardinia and Turkey, but in Spain and Sicily it can be made from larger, deepwater species (bluefin tuna and swordfish). Japanese cooks salt, press and sun-dry the roe of mullets into *karasumi*, and salt pollock roe to make *mentaiko*. *Myeongran* is a spicier Korean version of *botargo*, made either from mullet or Alaskan pollock. *Taramas* is a softer salted roe, made in Greece, from carp or cod. Smoked black – or striped – mullet is a regional speciality along Florida's Gulf coast. This fatty fish is often rubbed with hot spices before being smoked over wood from local trees (hickory, oak or orange). In northeast Africa, Egyptians salt and ferment sun-dried gray mullets to make *fesikh*, while expatriots substitute mullet for whitefish or shad in North America.

Jeotgal is a collective term for salted and fermented seafoods used in Korean cooking. They can be made from the flesh or roe of finfish, or from oysters, shrimp, other shellfish or even fish offal. *Gejang* (*gejeot*), for example, is Korean crab fermented with soya products as well as, or instead of, chillies. Like the fish sauces of Southeast Asia, *jeotgal* serves the same function as soy sauce, providing both salt and savour. The Cambodian fish paste *prahok*, a fermented mudfish (a type of snakehead fish), is a condiment for rice or a seasoning for meat dishes. Fermented ingredients like the ones listed here have been around for a long time – written references to them date at least to the third century BCE.

Racks used for smoking gepe roa, a kind of flying fish also known as ballyhoo (*Hemiramphus brasiliensis*). The photograph was taken in Manado, but the fish are caught in waters from Sulawesi to the Moluccas.

'Aunt Ola', a seller
of smoked skipjack,
in Manado,
Indonesia.

Smoked fufu, skipjack tuna (*Katsuwonus pelamis*). It's prepared this way all over eastern Indonesia, but especially in Bitung, North Sulawesi.

Japanese *shiokara* – a salty mixture of fish fermented in its own entrails, similar to *jeotgal* – is served in sake bars, but is usually consumed while drinking shots of Scotch whisky. Westerners might imagine that strong drink would indeed be essential both before and after ingesting a mouthful of decomposed fish guts, and apparently so do the Japanese. *Shiokara* is fermented, for a month or so, in a mixture of salt and *shio-koji* (rice malt), then packed in jars. They can be made from any number of marine creatures – chum salmon, cuttlefish, fiddler crabs, firefly squid, oysters, sea cucumbers, sea urchin roe or skipjack tuna.

The Chinese love dried seafood of all types – from shrimp to scallops to squid – but their most prized ingredient appears in shark's fin soup. Because of its expense and unusual texture, it has been a traditional part of festive dinners – such as weddings and state banquets – since the Ming Dynasty. Unfortunately, modern fishing techniques have led to severe over-fishing: studies show that millions of sharks are killed each year. Today, boycotts have reduced consumption to a fraction of what it had been, and many people are serving a kind of artificial shark's fin soup made with gelatine instead.[16]

Crustaceans

East, South and Southeast Asians have a long history – most of which did not include refrigeration – of using dried, salted or fermented seafood, including crustaceans. *Xiā mǐ* (literally 'shrimp rice') are tiny, dried shrimp that provide protein and a sweet savouriness to Chinese soups, sauces and noodle dishes. They are known as *bazun-chauk* in Myanmar, *ebi* in Indonesia, *hibi* in the Philippines and *kung haeng* in Thailand. Indians choose from three different types of dried shrimp, ranging from tiny (*javla*) to large. The latter are available either shelled (*soda*) or not (*sukat*). A taste for dried shrimp in Africa led to their appearance across the Atlantic (via the slave trade) in dishes from the northeast coast of Brazil to the Cajun cooking of Louisiana in the United States.

Fermented shrimp pastes add complex salty flavours to the dishes of southern China and Southeast Asia. They are known, variously, as *gaimbo* in India; *haam ha*, *ha jeung*, *hom ha* or *hae ko* in China; *kapi* in Cambodia, Thailand and Laos; *terasi* in Indonesia; *ngapi* in Myanmar; *mam ruốc*, *mam tép* and *mam tôm* in Vietnam; *bagoong alamang* or *bagoong aramang* in the Philippines; and *belacan*, *belachan*, *blachang* or *cincalok* in Malaysia. Small shrimp – *udang geragau* – combined with rice and salt are fermented in the sun for three days to produce Malaysian *cincalok*. The shrimp are not completely decomposed, giving the condiment a loose texture, more like a relish than a sauce. All of the pastes mentioned can be used while they are still moist from their curing jars, or sliced from firm, sun-dried blocks. Either way, they are quite pungent, and can be off-putting to unaccustomed noses. *Hae ko* is a black, sweetened form of shrimp paste with almost the consistency of molasses (which it resembles), and is used in the cuisines of Indonesia, Malaysia and Singapore.

Filipino cooks salt tiny freshwater crabs and press them into a paste – *taba ng talangka* – that has *botargo*-like pungency. In Thailand, small freshwater crabs, *boo kem*, ferment in brine to yield

Xiā mǐ – tiny dried shrimp no more than ¾ inch (19 mm) long – a common ingredient in Cantonese cooking.

two products: a kind of fish sauce and the salted crabs themselves. Koreans make several kinds of fermented crabs (collectively known as *gejang*), some eaten relatively fresh, but one called *cham-gejang gejang* is aged for a year or so. Crocks full of Chinese mitten crabs ferment in a mixture of chilli, garlic, ginger, spring onions, sesame oil and sugar.

For years, people went to great lengths to find ways to keep lobsters alive – up to the very minute when they are cooked – because

Eliza Leslie's Pickled Lobster (1840)

Take half a dozen fine lobsters. Put them into boiling salt and water, and when they are all done, take them out and extract all the meat from the shells, leaving that of the claws as whole as possible, and cutting the flesh of the body into large pieces nearly of the same size. Season a sufficient quantity of vinegar very highly with whole pepper-corns, whole cloves, and whole blades of mace. Put the pieces of lobster onto a stew-pan, and pour on just sufficient vinegar to keep them well covered. Set it over a moderate fire; and when it has boiled hard about five minutes, take out the lobster, and let the pickle boil by itself for a quarter of an hour. When the pickle and lobster are both cold, put them together into a broad flat stone jar. Cover it closely, and set it away in a cool place. Eat the pickled lobster with oil, mustard, and vinegar, and have bread and butter with it.[17]

the delicate flesh spoils so quickly. Today, restaurants – thousands of miles from any ocean – can be found with tanks of clattering crustacea. In the distant past, it was almost impossible to preserve lobster, but, by the seventeenth century, the British developed a taste for potted lobster:

Cooked lobster meat was covered in butter in a stoneware crock and kept cold. As with cold fish pies sealed in butter, such dishes could last up to a year, making it possible to carry preserved lobster . . . further inland. Potted lobster

Potted Lobster (mid-19th century)

Parboil the lobster in boiling water well salted. Then pick out all the meat from the body and claws, and beat it in a mortar with nutmeg, mace, cayenne, and salt, to your taste. Beat the coral separately. Then put the pounded meat into a large potting can of block tin with a cover. Press it down hard, having arranged it in alternate layers of white meat and coral to give it a marbled or variegated appearance. Cover it with fresh butter, and put it into a slow oven for half an hour. When cold, take off the butter and clarify it, by putting it into a jar, which, must be set in a pan of boiling water.

Watch it well, and when it melts, carefully skim off the buttermilk which will rise to the top. When no more scum rises, take it off and let it stand for a few minutes to settle, and then strain it through a sieve. Put the lobster into small potting-cans, pressing it down very hard. Pour the clarified butter over it, and secure the covers tightly. Potted lobster is used to lay between thin slices of bread as sandwiches. The clarified butter that accompanies it is excellent for fish sauce. Prawns and crabs may be potted in a similar manner.[18]

was savoured throughout the 1700s, and recipes for it eventually appeared in America.[19]

These recipes are obviously for lobsters from northern waters – American and European lobsters. With the advent of flash freezing and high-speed travel in the mid-twentieth century, tropical, spiny lobsters from Australia, the Caribbean, New Zealand and South Africa became available in Europe and the U.S. Spiny lobsters lack the huge claws of their northern relatives, so their meaty tails are the only parts shipped. Frozen lobster tails are perfect for restaurants – no waste, no worry about spoilage and portion size tends to be quite uniform, so cooking time and profit margin are easily controlled. It is therefore no accident that many restaurants, especially chain restaurants – where uniformity and convenience are commercial virtues – include more lobster tails than whole live lobsters on their menus.

Molluscs and Gastropods

Molluscs such as clams, mussels, scallops, oysters and cockles are generally consumed fresh, but may be preserved by pickling, freezing or canning. Canned clams, as well as bottled clam broth, cans of oyster stew and clam chowders of several descriptions, sit in our kitchen cabinets, ready to be opened. Little tins of smoked oysters are more likely found in the 'gourmet' section of a grocer's aisles. Chinese markets abound with dried and salted molluscs, such as *gān bèi* or *conpoy* (scallops), either loose in barrels or packaged in ubiquitous cellophane bags. Most of the 'fresh' scallops sold in fish markets are shipped frozen, and sometimes pre-treated with sodium tripolyphosphate (STPP), a chemical that causes scallops to gain weight by absorbing water. Most cockles are eaten fresh, but pickled cockles – many of them from Morecambe Bay, on the northwest coast of England – are sold in jars or snack-sized plastic bags.

Gastropods, a huge class of molluscs, can be found in, or near, fresh or salt water. Many are among the most prized of human foods, often closely associated with specific localities: just think of the *escargots* of France, the *scungilli* of Italy, the conches of the Caribbean or the abalone of the Pacific coasts. Abalone is a luxury food that has been seriously over-fished in many places. California, for example, has placed strict limits on sport diving for wild abalone, none of which may be sold. Commercially legal 'American' abalone is farm-raised, and much of it comes from northern Japan; it is canned and shipped from Hawaii. Elsewhere, various restrictions apply, which has created extensive black markets for this ocean creature. Illegally collected South African abalone is frequently exported to Asian countries where it is almost as prized as shark's fins. Chinese *guàntóu bàoyú* (canned abalone), from Australia or Mexico, comes in tins or small shelf-stable plastic tubs. The brine-packed abalone needs no refrigeration. Some abalone is frozen, but Chinese gastronomes prefer the complex flavours of *bao yu*, the dried adductor muscle. Several types of marine snails are eaten by humans, from tiny periwinkles to the larger whelks (Buccinidae family) that provide conch and *scungilli*. Conch is usually eaten fresh in the Caribbean and South America, but slices of dried conch (*lúo ròu* in Chinese) are shipped from Latin America to China. Dormant garden snails – *escargots* – that appear to be dried are actually alive and need only to be refreshed in water to revive. As their preparation is fairly tedious, many people simply use canned snails, often sold with already cleaned shells to enable the simulation of the fresh gourmet dish.

Cephalopods

Cephalopods constitute a limited 'family' of foodstuffs. We eat only three types: cuttlefish, octopi and squid. Of these soft-bodied creatures, squid are the most commonly consumed. Curiously, their soft flesh becomes tough and chewy if not properly prepared – but that very chewiness is regarded as a positive feature among Asian consumers for whom texture is as important as flavour.

Dried squid, shredded or whole, are a popular ingredient in East Asian cookery, although the smell of dried seafood can be distressing to unaccustomed noses. In Hawaii, Japan and Korea, they are often eaten, without further preparation, as a salty, chewy snack food. In Hawaii, small snack-sized packages of dried squid, *saki ika*, come in two flavours: 'regular' or 'hot' – the latter may be dusted with cayenne, but is more sweet than fiery. They are generally processed with various sweeteners, such as sorbitol, and MSG. A Korean side dish, *ojingeochae bokkeum*, is shredded dry squid cooked in chilli-laced *gochujang* and sugar.

Cuttlefish are used in several Mediterranean cuisines, often because of their sepia – a kind of ink they produce to hide from predators. Squid and octopi produce smaller quantities of this ink. Black ink-dyed rice dishes are made in Croatia, Italy and Spain – but the best-known food incorporating sepia is dried pasta, especially dishes featuring elegant and dramatically black linguine made with squid ink. Dried octopus (*polbo*) used to be a staple, like stockfish, in the interior of the Iberian Peninsula, but frozen octopus has largely replaced it. Even in American fish stores, canned or frozen octopus is seen more often than fresh, since the demand for it is low outside 'ethnic' markets.

Poultry

Poultry, like seafood, is very perishable. It can be dried into jerky (I have even tried ostrich jerky) but it is only safe to do so after the meat has been heated to 72°C (160°F) to kill any bacteria – especially the dreaded *E. coli* and *Salmonella*. Poultry sausages are popular among cultures that eschew pork. Sausages of chicken, duck and goose require curing salts that contain nitrites and/

or nitrates. This is a lesson not learned by the producers of one particularly frightening form of preserved poultry, *kiviak*:

> A delicacy among Inuit people of Greenland, it consists of placing a dead auk (a kind of gull resembling a penguin) in sealskin and burying it for some seven months – until it is fully rotted. The result is a stinky dish with a slightly sweet flavor.[20]

This short description does not begin to express the horrors of this traditional Inuit treat. First, it is not just one auk, but 300 to 400 of the round little birds. They are placed whole (beaks, feathers and entrails) inside a raw sealskin, stitched up tight, sealed with melted seal fat and buried – which explains the air-less conditions so favourable to *C. botulinum*. After the package is exhumed and a bird is removed, its head is pulled off and the bitter entrails are squeezed out, before the rest is then eaten (*sans* feathers) raw. The result is said to be no worse than a stinky over-ripened cheese – but it sounds like an unholy cross between *garum* and *confit d'oie*.

French confit is a much safer and presumably tastier way to preserve poultry (we have not made – and are extremely unlikely to make – a comparative taste test). Traditionally, the tougher parts – legs and even gizzards – of ducks, geese and also chickens or turkeys, are slowly simmered in fat, at temperatures between 72 and 85°C (160 and 185°F). They are packed in ceramic pots and sealed under a layer of air-excluding fat. Fat keeps well unrefriger-ated so long as it is free of water. Succulent confit can be stored for months in a cool pantry.

Gelatine excludes air as effectively as fat but must be kept cold to prevent melting. Headcheese, and its vinegary cousin souse, are perfect examples. The proteinaceous liquid – sufficiently reduced and clarified – sets into a firm jelly, hermetically sealing the other ingredients in a translucent, sliceable matrix.

Canning is safer for poultry, but the high temperatures required to destroy *C. botulinum*'s spores ultimately change the meat's flavour and texture (and not for the better). By far the best methods for preserving poultry involve cold. Freezing is the obvious choice for long-term storage, but many people object to changes in texture, especially if the meat is not frozen quickly enough to prevent the formation of large ice crystals. Frozen chickens can be stored for twelve months at -18°C (-0.4°F) and for 24 months between

To Souce a Capon (1839)

Take a good bodied Capon, young, fat, and finely pulled, drawn and trussed, lay it in soak two or three hours with a knuckle of veal well joynted, and after set them a boiling in a fine deep brass-pan, kettle, or large pipkin, in a gallon of fair water; when it boils, scum it, and put in four or five blades of mace, two or three races of ginger slic't, four fennil-roots, and four parsley-roots, scraped and picked, and salt. The Capon being fine and tender boild take it up, and put it in other warm liquor or broth, then put to your souced broth a quart of white-wine, and boil it to a jelly; then take it off, and put it into an earthen pan or large pipkin, put your capon to it, with two or three slic't lemons, and cover it close, serve it at your pleasure, and garnish it with slices and pieces of lemon, barberries, roots, mace, nutmeg, and some of the jelly.

Some put to this souc't capon, whole pepper, & a faggot of sweet herbs, but that maketh the broth very black.

In that manner you may souce any Land Fowl.[21]

-25°C (-13°F) and -30°C (-22°F), but such low temperatures are well below the capacity of most home freezers.

What many shoppers do not realize is that the 'fresh' poultry they find in the markets is not truly fresh. The cleaned carcasses are almost frozen, either in a cooling tunnel or a bath of ice water, to reduce their body heat to safe levels. The meat is then held, for at least a few days, at 0°C (32°F) – but no lower than -1°C (-2°F) to avoid the potential damage of freezing. The resting period allows the enzymes in the flesh to cause it to 'ripen', effectively tenderizing the meat.

Grains and Pulses

Grains and pulses (or legumes) were probably the earliest foods committed to long storage. The only requirement for their storage was dry, well-circulating air and a vermin-free location. However, our ancestors quickly learned that some processing could make these simply preserved foods much more nutritious and appetizing.

If the seeds of grain are allowed to sprout, some very desirable chemical reactions, called malting, occur. Various enzymes – primarily amylase, formed by the newly developing seedling – convert complex carbohydrates (starches) into simpler ones, providing usable energy that the plant can use for growth. Those simpler carbohydrates (sugars) include glucose, maltose, maltotriose and a few more complex sugars called maltodextrines. Proteases, also present in the grain, are enzymes that convert some of the protein into sugars. If heated at just the right moment (when the maximum amount of sugars have been created, but before the young plant has begun to consume them), several things happen: the seedling dies, so no sugar goes to waste; the enzymes are denatured, stopping all chemical activity; the heat destroys any other organisms that might want to consume the newly made sugars; and various chemical reactions form new flavouring compounds. Grains become tastier and sweeter (which is desirable if we want to use them to make Hershey's Whoppers, Maltesers, Ovaltine or a malted milkshake). While this appeals to our sweet teeth, those sugars are even more attractive to yeast (specifically, *Saccharomyces cerevisiae*).

Yeast wants to steal our sugar and convert it into waste – but that waste is ethyl alcohol. The resulting solution of alcohol and water can be distilled, eliminating much of the water, to produce various types of whiskies (depending on the type of grain and brewing or storage techniques used), vodkas and gins. If the original alcohol/water solution is bottled before the fermentation is complete, carbon dioxide (another of yeast's waste products) dissolves into the liquid under its own pressure. When the pressure is released, the CO_2 will turn back into a gas in the form of bubbles. The result? The foamy head on beer, or flute of sparkling champagne.

Sake, which despite being called 'rice wine' is more like beer, does not utilize malting to turn starch into fermentable sugars. Cooked rice ferments twice: initially by mould, *Aspergillus oryzae*, which breaks complex carbohydrates, starches, into simpler sugars; then *S. cerevisiae* ferments those sugars into alcohol. Most sake is pasteurized to stop the process and stabilize the product, which is why sake is not effervescent.

While there is some argument about whether leavened bread or beer brewing was invented first, a lot of grain goes into alcohol production. Mesoamericans were not growing the wheat, rye or barley of Europe or the rice of Asia. A wild grass, *teosinte*, domesticated before recorded history, became corn, or maize. It grows taller and faster and its 'ears' contain more grains (or 'kernels') that are larger and contain more edible starch than those of wild *teosinte*. Unfortunately for us, corn's proteins do not provide all of the amino acids we need. That deficiency causes kwashiorkor, a form of malnutrition. Fortunately, it is easily prevented by consuming beans, which – conveniently – are also native to the area in which Mesoamericans lived. Also corn's niacin comes in a form that cannot be used by humans, as it causes a deficiency disease.

Advertisement for Pabst Malt Extract, *c.* 1897.

Dyspepsia and Indigestion.....

There are times when the brain draws so upon our vitality that we cannot digest our food, we can get no strength from what we eat. If we let this go on, we sow the seeds of weakness which will blossom in disease. Read this letter about

PABST MALT EXTRACT
The "Best" Tonic.

If you are a brain worker, a woman with household worries and cares, or if you need physical strength to fight the battles of life,

act at once.
••••●●●••••

"I cannot be too grateful for the immense improvement PABST MALT EXTRACT, the "Best" Tonic, has made in my system. Two years ago I was a dyspeptic wreck of fifty, but PABST MALT EXTRACT, The "Best" Tonic, has changed all that. It has not only cured my dyspepsia, but it has braced my nerves and cured me completely of insomnia. I consider that it has saved my life. It has changed a nervous, broken down wreck of fifty-two to a strong, fresh young man of forty. When my daughter was recovering from typhoid fever, she gained nearly a pound a day for three weeks, solely by the liberal use of your decidedly "Best" Tonic.

JOHN D. HOMER, Haywards, Cal.

ASK FOR "PABST"

PERFECTION IN BREWING IS REACHED IN AMERICA

THE FIRST INAUGURATION

BINNER CHICAGO

Over 3,000 years ago, Mesoamericans discovered nixtamalization – a method of treating dried corn with strong alkalis (calcium hydroxide from limestone or the burned shells of molluscs; potassium hydroxide from wood and ash; and in some places, naturally occurring sodium hydroxide). Nixtamalization made it easy to remove the indigestible pericarp, the outer layer of the kernels, but, more significantly, it converted the corn's niacin into a form our systems could use. Many early European colonists ignored Native Americans' advice about treating corn with alkali, and suffered the deficiency disease pellagra as a result. The problem persisted among the poor in the southern U.S. well into the last century. Since then, niacin-enriched wheat flour in cornbread has largely eliminated pellagra among affected populations, although elsewhere, in parts of Africa and the Indian subcontinent, the problem of pellagra has yet to diminish.

Canned hominy, nixtamalized field corn.

Nixtamalized corn takes many forms. The simplest is hominy: large, softened and skinless kernels of dried corn. The dried corn, available in cans or dried, is soaked overnight before simmering in an alkaline solution. In Mexico, it is known simply as *maiz pozolero*, and can be eaten, as is, in soups and stews such as *menudo* or *posole*. Fresh nixtamal, made without pre-soaking, and with some of the skins left on, can be ground and kneaded into *masa* dough. Masa is used to make *arepas* (soft sweet corn cakes, also called *gorditas* and *pupusas*), tamales and tortillas. If the nixtamal is first dried, then ground, it becomes *masa harina*, which does not spoil and is easily reconstituted with a little water. Dried hominy may be whole,

or ground in varying textures, such as cornmeal and grits. Milled hominy yields cornbread in the U.S., *harapash* in Albania, *congee* in China, *cou-cou* in Barbados and various forms of *fufu*, *nshima*, *pap* and *ugali* across several African countries. The term 'cornflour' refers to any finely ground cornmeal in the U.S, but only to cornstarch in the UK.

Aside from its primary use as flour, wheat becomes a preserved food in the form of dried pasta and couscous. Historically, most Italian households took their wheat in the form of a porridge that had not changed much since the Romans made *pulmentum* (which became polenta after maize was introduced). Dried pasta was too labour-intensive for everyday consumption and was reserved instead for special occasions. Only when pasta could be mass-produced, by dough-extruding machines in the nineteenth century, did it become the staple it is today. Couscous, on the other hand, could easily be made, dried and stored for travel. It is essentially a firm dough made with semolina (a hard, high-gluten wheat flour) and water. Instead of being rolled and cut – like other pastas – the dough is grated into tiny pellets, then steamed immediately or left to dry for future use. The 'grain' size of couscous varies from place to place. The largest, consisting of little balls of rolled dough dried by roasting, was created during a rice shortage in Israel during the 1950s. It is a relatively recent invention; fine-grained Arabic versions date at least to the thirteenth century.

Wheat is not just a starchy staple (or source of alcohols, like Bavarian *Weissbiers*). It is higher in protein than any other major grain. Wheat is the primary ingredient in

Korn-Krisp ad from *Cosmopolitan* magazine in 1902. 'Delicious but Vitalizing. Nutritious but not Fattening. Nerve Building but not Heating.'

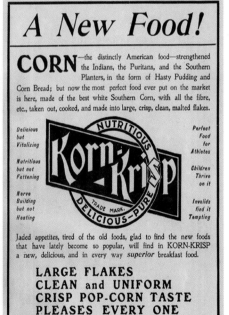

A New Food!

CORN —the distinctly American food—strengthened the Indians, the Puritans, and the Southern Planters, in the form of Hasty Pudding and Corn Bread; but now the most perfect food ever put on the market is here, made of the best white Southern Corn, with all the fibre, etc., taken out, cooked, and made into large, crisp, clean, malted flakes.

Delicious but Vitalizing

Nutritious but not Fattening

Nerve Building but not Heating

Perfect Food for Athletes

Children Thrive on it

Invalids find it Tempting

Jaded appetites, tired of the old foods, glad to find the new foods that have lately become so popular, will find in KORN-KRISP a new, delicious, and in every way *superior* breakfast food.

**LARGE FLAKES
CLEAN and UNIFORM
CRISP POP-CORN TASTE
PLEASES EVERY ONE**

FAR MORE NOURISHING THAN WHEAT
MUCH LESS STARCH THAN WHEAT
35% MORE BRAIN and NERVE FOOD THAN OATMEAL

many ready-to-eat breakfast cereals, products that are among the most successful sellers of all mass-marketed prepared foods. A Battle Creek competitor of Dr John Harvey Kellogg developed a cereal based on wheat. In 1897 Charles William 'C. W.' Post formulated a granular cereal (as opposed to the earlier flakes produced by Kellogg) made from a baked batter of wheat and malted barley. He called it 'Grape Nuts', despite it containing neither ingredient. Post and Kellogg were not, however, the first to make a ready-to-eat breakfast cereal. That honour belongs to Henry Drushel Perky, who in 1892 created a cereal he first called 'Muffets', then renamed 'Shredded Wheat'.

Wheat is also the base of fermented sauces, such as the soy sauce family, in China. It serves as a thickener for many Western soups and sauces, such as gravies and the classical French sauces *velouté* and *béchamel*, and wheat starch serves the same purpose in thousands of mass-produced prepared foods.

Rice, like wheat and corn, has been made into breakfast cereals, but unlike them it is also made into the milk that goes into the bowl. Rice, like soybeans and nuts, can be ground and processed with water to make milk substitutes for vegans, and people who are either lactose-intolerant or have allergies to milk proteins. The enzymatic conversion of starches provides their milky sweetness. Rice's starch is nearly all amylopectin, which gelatinizes very easily when heated. It is the basis of several Asian snack foods; Japanese *mochi* is typical. It begins with cooked short-grain rice pounded into a smooth gelatinous mass. *Mochi* is formed into cakes filled with various sweet pastes to make confections called *wagashi* (Indonesian *kue moci* is similar). *Mochi* can be filled with peanut pureé and rolled in sesame seeds, layered in tri-coloured rhomboids (*hishi mochi*), rolled into little ice-cream-filled bonbons or fried in small balls called *arare*.

Rice noodles are very popular in China and all over Southeast Asia. Fresh rice noodles can sometimes be found, but are more commonly bought dried. These are made by grinding short-grain rice in water, and strained to remove any residual solids. The resulting 'dough' is smoother and more translucent than *mochi*. The noodles are rolled, formed into desired shapes and dried.

East Asians make crackers from cooked, puffed or fried rice (or some combination of methods): Indonesian *krupuk* and *rengginang*; Japanese *senbei*; Javanese *intip*; and Vietnamese *co'm cháy*. Airy and flavourless – but low-calorie – puffed rice cakes are joylessly consumed in the U. S. and Canada by dieters (presumably to help them lose all interest in eating).

Barley is an ancient foodstuff; it was important in Mesopotamia, especially after intensive irrigation left soils too salty to grow wheat. We eat only small amounts of barley today; instead, we prefer to drink it. Malted barley starch, in the form of fermented sugars, has inebriated innumerable generations with beer and distilled potables, such as Irish and Scotch whiskies. Barley comes in three forms: one with two rows of grains on each spike; one with six rows; and an unhulled variety that is mainly used as animal feed. Two-row barley has a higher starch-to-protein ratio than other varieties, so is used to produce top-fermented English-style ales and German beers, which are brewed warm, thus creating complex flavours and aromas. Lagers, which dominate the American beer market, are bottom-fermented and cold. They use six-row barley and sometimes corn and rice, yielding less flavourful brews that require more hops. Malted barley can also be made into less potent beverages. It is toasted until dark brown, developing new flavours due to Maillard reactions, then ground to make the misleadingly named Italian beverage *caffè d'orzo*, which is not coffee; nor is it made from rice, or even rice-shaped pasta.

Despite these other uses, barley hasn't completely disappeared from our menus. Barley flour and meal are still used in baking, and as breakfast porridge in northern regions of the United Kingdom. Since the nineteenth century, potatoes have largely replaced barley in Central Europe – except for dried pearl barley, which still appears in soups. The region's

Cover of a promotional booklet for Shredded Wheat, 1928.

Cereal ad from 1902, with a testimonial from Chas. A. Minks, MD, of the Board of Health, Fall River, Massachusetts: 'Cook's Flaked Rice is the cleanest and purest food product I ever saw.'

Ashkenazi Jews have kept barley in their cuisine wherever the diaspora has taken them.

Oats, like barley, feed more animals than humans. Samuel Johnson (who didn't think much of oats, nor, for that matter, of his neighbours to the north), defined oats as 'A grain which in England is generally given to horses, but in Scotland supports the people.' Oats are still eaten by humans, but only in very specific ways. Oats combine with various forms of offal in Scottish haggis, but, elsewhere, oatmeal cookies (with or without raisins) are a childhood staple, as is a hot bowl of oatmeal porridge at breakfast. Porridge has very different properties depending on which side of the Atlantic it is prepared. American oats are steamed before rolling, which softens them, making them less likely to shatter into meal, and they retain some texture after cooking. The oats for Irish and Scottish porridge are not steamed, but finely ground, leading to a smoother, more uniform porridge. Either way, the oats are heated before milling to prolong their shelf-life, denaturing the enzymes in the grain that would allow oils to become rancid. Oats find their way into cold breakfast cereals as well, such as granola (which is baked with honey, oil and several other grains and seeds) and muesli (containing nuts and dried fruit). Like barley, oats can be sprouted and malted for use in brewing. These malts produce a beer that has a fuller, creamier mouthfeel. They tend to be darkly roasted, producing stouts and porters, which are rich, deep-flavoured brews with high alcohol contents.

Rye thrives in cooler, damper climates than wheat, so it is commonly grown in northern Europe and Canada. It is almost always used in some fermented form, such as whiskey or sourdough breads, or as *zur* – a thick, fermented, almost porridge-like soup from Poland.

'Millet' is a collective term for several species of grasses, from four different genera (*Echinochloa*, *Panicum*, *Pennisetum* and *Setaria*) indigenous to Africa and Asia. They have been grown since prehistoric times, for over ten millennia. In fact, in China they were originally a more significant crop than rice. In the developed world today, most of the millet crop goes into birdseed, with only a tiny amount sold for human consumption – mostly in health food stores. Millet seeds are quite small, which is part of the reason they are not used more widely today. Nonetheless, in Africa and parts of India, millet outproduces other grains due to its tolerance for semi-arid conditions and its quick yields, and makes up a greater part of the diet.

Like other starchy grains, millet is fermented to make alcohol. Millet beers are made in Taiwan and in Africa (in combination with sorghum). In Nepal and northern India, millet is cooked, then inoculated with *murcha*, a mixture of bacteria, moulds and yeast. After fermentation, the brew is sealed and aged for six months. The result is beer-like *chhaang*, or *tongba*, that is drunk hot. These brews can also be distilled to make a much stronger Nepalese or Tibetan drink, *raksi*. A similar drink, *ara*, is sometimes made from millet in Bhutan (though corn, rice and wheat are more commonly employed). *Bragă*, a thick millet-based beverage from Romania, is sometimes flavoured with dehydrated *kvass*, hops and sweet syrup. Teff (*Eragrostis tef*) is called 'Ethiopian millet' in France, though it only resembles millet in having tiny seeds. It is best known in the form of the traditional Ethiopian and Eritrean bread *injera* – a large crêpe-like bread made of fermented teff flour. Communal meals are served on a large *injera*, with diners scooping up bits of food in torn pieces of the *injera* in place of utensils. The sauce-soaked trencher is eaten at the end of the meal.

Sorghum (the grain has the same name as the genus), or milo, is a grass related to sugar cane. In fact, one species, *Sorghum bicolour*, can be grown either for its grain (for animal feed) or for its sap, which can be boiled to yield 'sorghum molasses'. Like other sugar sources, sorghum can be fermented to produce alcohol. Much of that ethanol is burned as fuel – but the Chinese distil high-powered *baijiu* from sorghum.

Beans can be divided, for our purposes, into two categories: those from the Old World and those from the New. Very few are consumed as a 'fresh' vegetable (such as *haricots verts*); they are more frequently canned or frozen, and most often dried before any other use. Drying is certainly the oldest, and still the most common, form of preservation of legumes. The Old World varieties include soya beans, which are certainly the most used, and most-often preserved, legumes in the world. They were first grown in East Asia some 5,000 years ago, but began to be grown throughout the world during the nineteenth century. Preserved soya products will be covered in much more detail later. Mung beans, or *moong dal* (*Vigna radiata*), originated in India, where they are hulled and dried. Elsewhere, they are more familiar as sprouts. These sprouts (as well as those of soybeans) are widely consumed throughout East and Southeast Asia, where they are sold fresh or in cans. Mung bean starch is used to make 'cellophane noodles' and Chinese and Korean jellies (*liangfen* and *nokdumuk*, respectively). East Asian adzuki beans (*Vigna angularis*) have been domesticated for at least 6,000 years. Sometimes eaten whole, they are more often used in the form of sweetened bean pastes, such as the filling for Chinese mooncakes, or to sweeten iced tea in Hong Kong. The Japanese love adzuki-based sweets: baked or boiled buns (*anpan*, *dorayaki*, *imagawayaki*, *manjū* and *taiyaki*); a kind of stuffed cookie (*monaka*); and candies (*amanattō*, *daifuku*). Adzuki bean paste is as familiar in the East as chocolate is in the West. Red bean ice cream, for example, is the favoured flavour throughout the Pacific region.

Fava beans, or broad beans (*Vicia faba*), have been a Mediterranean mainstay for 8,000 years. Indigenous from North Africa to India, they were among the earliest domesticated plants. They are fried and salted, and sometimes dosed with chilli powder, as ready-made snack foods in China, Colombia, Guatemala, Iran, Malaysia, Mexico, Peru and Thailand. In Ethiopia, favas are ground into *shiro*, a kind of flour used to thicken stew-like *wats*.

Lentils (*Lens culinaris*) have been eaten as early as the Neolithic age, some 13,000 years ago. Lentils come in several colours, with or without their hulls, but are always dried. Brown lentils are the most common variety in the West, except in France, where tiny round green lentils are preferred. South Asians use both the brown-skinned ones and hulled red lentils. Tiny black lentils are sometimes called 'beluga lentils' because of their resemblance to the expensive caviar. Lentils are deficient in two of the amino acids – cysteine and methionine – needed for human nutrition, unless they are sprouted. Yoghurt, another preserved ingredient common in Indian and Middle Eastern cuisines, provides enough to balance even unsprouted lentils. They are commonly eaten with grains, in soups or as thick purées: the *dals* of Bangladesh, India, Nepal, Pakistan, Sri Lanka and the West Indies, or the *wats* of Ethiopia.

Peas (*Pisum sativum*) are sometimes called 'English peas' to help distinguish them from other 'peas', which we will address shortly. Peas are consumed in various stages of their development: the young shoots are eaten; fresh, immature pods (snow peas and sugar snaps) may be fresh or frozen; more mature seeds are available fresh, canned or frozen; and fully mature seeds are dried. Dried peas have been a staple for a long time – they have been part of the human diet for at least 7,000 years. The medieval nursery rhyme 'pease porridge hot, pease porridge cold, pease porridge in the pot, nine days old', gives a hint of their longevity, albeit in a less than appetizing manner. The dried, hulled seeds we call 'split peas', however, had to wait another two centuries. They come in green and yellow varieties (American split pea soup is usually green, while the Canadian version is more likely to be yellow). Peas, today, have taken on new lives as snack foods. Salted peas are popular in Southeast Asia, and cooked and dried peas – coated with wasabi, or a wasabi-like paste of horseradish, mustard and green food-colouring – have moved beyond Japan's immense snack market to the rest of the world.

Chickpeas (*Cicer arietinum*) have been welcome on our tables for nearly 8,000 years, as reflected by their many names: India's *chana* and *sanagalu*, Italian *ceci* and Spanish *garbanzo*. The Arabic name for chickpeas, *hummus*, is also the name for the most famous dish incorporating them. Never seen by the average consumer fresh, they are sold dried or in cans. Dried, peeled and split Indian chickpeas are *chana dal* (a name for both the ingredient and the dish). Dried chickpea flour is the basis of *falafel* – a dish that has been made all over the Middle East for so long that every country claims to have originated it. A kind of tofu is even made from chickpeas in Myanmar. While most chickpea dishes are savoury, Filipinos preserve them in heavy syrup for dessert, and Bangladeshis make a kind of halvah, called *uter halua*, from them.

Pigeon peas (*Cajanus cajan*) originated in India – where they are called *toor dal* – but arrived in Africa thousands of years ago. Only a few centuries ago, they came to the New World along with the slave trade. Much of the world's crop go to animal feed, but people eat them too, either fresh, canned or dried. Dried ones are sometimes ground into flour or sprouted. Pigeon peas are especially associated with the Caribbean, Latin America and Hawaii, where various forms of rice and beans are staple foods.

Black-eyed peas (or black-eyed beans, *Vigna unguiculata*) are sometimes called 'cow peas', which probably began as a way of denigrating them as unsuitable for the refined tastes of slave-owners, but not the slaves who brought them from Africa. Africans had used these legumes in fritters, showing the influence of Islam in the region, and Nigerians still make *abará*, a fermented paste of the de-skinned peas. The idea of *abará* travelled to Brazil as well, where it was transformed into a dish resembling tamales. Union troops, during America's Civil War, didn't even bother to destroy fields of black-eyed peas because they did not consider them to be food for humans and had not realized that these peas had become an essential part of the menu in southern states. They are so dominant that in Texas they are simply called 'peas' (if Texans want those little green things that Yankees eat, they have to specify 'English peas'). Other than during the brief period when they are ripe for the picking, these 'peas' are always used dried, and usually cooked along with another southern staple: cured and/or smoked pork, in the form of bacon, fatback or hambones.

Hoppin' John (dried black-eyed peas, rice and salt pork) is served, for good luck, on New Year's Day in the southern United States. Food traditions like this utilize preserved foods to retain continuity with the past. In fact, the custom of using dried legumes to welcome in the New Year is much older than the American slave era. It might even be older than the holiday that begins our calendars. Something similar (about serving them, for luck, on *Rosh Hashana*) appeared some 1,500 years ago in the *Talmud*. Whether it was a result of a mistranslation or not, it had become an accepted part of Sephardic Jewish culture by the sixteenth century and remains so to this day. *Sekihan*, a Japanese mixture of white rice and tiny dried red azuki beans, is often served at New Year's, curiously mirroring the Hoppin' John tradition. Dried lentils, on New Year's Day, are believed to bring coins to those who eat them at many Mediterranean tables.

Seeds, other than grains or legumes, are often dried, ground to powders, or – if their fat content is sufficiently high – milled into pastes or oils. Sesame seeds (*Sesamum indicum*) are a perfect example. They are pressed to make two different oils: raw seeds make a light, mild oil suitable for cooking, while toasted seeds yield a flavourful oil (*ma you*) used in Chinese dishes. The dark oil, sometimes called 'gingelly', is easily burned, so is not used for frying; it is added near the end of cooking, or as a garnish, to provide a rich nutty taste. Sesame seeds are also ground into two kinds of pastes: the raw – or lightly toasted – seeds make *tahini*, a staple in Middle Eastern dishes, like *hummus* (a pureé of chickpeas, garlic and lemon juice). A darker and more fragrant Chinese sesame paste (*zhi ma jiang*) is made from heavily toasted seeds.

Mustard seeds have some curious properties. Their hot flavours are due to the presence of isothiocyanate compounds that

exist only as potential in the seeds. Two different precursors (myronate and myrasin), one in the seed itself and the other an enzyme in the husk of the seed, need to be combined in the presence of water for the isothiocyanates to form. When the seeds are heated, their denatured enzymes cannot develop the desired burning taste. Toasted mustard seeds contribute a nutty richness, but not heat, to some Indian dishes. Even the heat created by friction while grinding the seeds can denature the enzyme. Maurice Grey invented a kind of mill, in 1777, that did not overheat the seeds. He later joined with Auguste Poupon to market their prepared mustard.

Pungent mustard oil provides one of the flavourings in Indian *achars*, sharp-tasting pickles loaded with chillies and salt. Rapeseed, a relative of mustard, has yielded cooking oil since the nineteenth century – but it contained glucosinolates and erucic acid that gave it a pungent and bitter flavour. New varieties developed in the 1980s reduced the concentrations of these compounds, making the oil more palatable. The new oil has a high smoke-point, so foods can be fried at high temperatures, leading to crisper, less greasy products. Canada is the second-largest producer of edible rapeseed oil after China, which explains its commercial name, 'canola', a contraction of 'Canadian oil'.

Mustard can label, late 19th century. The directions specify reconstituting with boiled and cooled water – which is correct, if for the wrong reason.

One of the least expensive edible oils is made from cottonseed. It has a neutral flavour and a high smoke point of 216°C (420°F), making it a bland but convenient product. It also contains enough tocopherol (vitamin E) to give it a long shelf-life, as it is a natural antioxidant. By minimizing losses due to product ageing, Con-Agra's Wesson has been able to convert a by-product of cotton production into a household commodity.

Not often thought of as 'seeds', coffee and chocolate are among the world's most consumed seeds (other than grains and legumes) and *only* in preserved form. Coffee cherries are often fermented to break down the fruit pulp and parchment-like covering on the beans, making them easier to remove. Care must be taken not to over-ferment, because the beans can develop a sour taste resembling old onions. The green beans are then dried to 12 per cent moisture content for storage. Cocoa beans undergo a more complex series of processes, without which the beans would have very little flavour. Yeasts first ferment the fruit that surrounds the beans, producing alcohol, which is then converted to acetic and lactic acids by bacteria. The aerobic bacteria that make acetic acid gradually increase the temperature of the rotting fruit, first killing the lactobacilli, then the cocoa bean itself. Once that happens, a series of decomposition reactions take place that reduce the beans' proteins into their constituent amino acids. This controlled decay actually produces the complex flavours and aromas we recognize as chocolate.

Dairy and Eggs

Milk is the first food we experience, albeit in the freshest form imaginable. It is also quite perishable, so adults who can digest the lactose in milk products have had to develop many ways to preserve them. Before refrigeration (and more modern techniques) were available, our ancestors created a wide range of methods and a rich variety of dairy foods: from liquid, to powdery dry, to as durable as stone; and from sweet to tangy, with every conceivable variation in between. Some are bland enough for infants, while others are so pungent that it can be an ordeal to sit in the same room with them.

Processed dairy products (butter, cheese and yoghurt) make perishable milk last longer. Most, even if fermented, still require some refrigeration, although canned and dehydrated forms can last for years. Since condensed milk inventor Gail Borden's time, dehydrated milk has been available to us, but we rarely use it as milk; it is generally a component of other, usually processed foods. If we use any powdered 'milk' at home, it is more likely to be a 'non-dairy creamer', which, despite its name, generally contains sodium caseinate (a soluble protein derived from milk).

Today, some whole milk is pasteurized at ultra-high temperatures of 130°C (282°F) and sealed in light-proof aseptic containers. This shelf-stable product requires no refrigeration and can last for six months – at least until opened, after which it must be refrigerated, like any other milk.

To Preserve Cream, and Syrup of Cream (1827)

Cream already skimmed may be preserved sweet, for twenty-four hours. Scald it, then add as much double re-fined sugar as will make it pretty sweet, then set in a cool place. Syrup of cream may be prepared in the same way; putting one pound and a quarter of sugar to a pint of fresh cream, set it away in a cool place for three hours; have ready nice two-ounce phials, and, after filling, cork close, and tie down with leather. Thus prepared, it will remain good for two weeks. This is excellent for a voyage to sea.[22]

Historically, fluid milk has been preserved (for only a short time) by fermentation. Lactobacilli are the primary fermenting agents for a spectrum of yoghurt-like beverages, such as *lassi*, an Indian mixture that may be flavoured with some combination of honey, spices and fruit; *kefir*, originally a Turkish product, then popular among Slavic peoples and now a global phenomenon; and the less widespread *kumiss*, fermented mare's milk from Central Asia. *Kefir* and *kumiss* differ from other yoghurt-like drinks, as they are fermented by a combination of lactobacilli and yeasts. They still have the same lactic-acid tang, but also a small kick of alcohol. *Kumiss* has a slightly higher alcohol content than *kefir*, because mare's milk contains more fermentable lactose than other milks. When mare's milk is unavailable for brewing *kumiss*, a small amount of sucrose is added to cow's milk.

Magazine advertisement for Borden's Peerless Brand Evaporated Cream, *c.* 1898.

Yoghurt has been around for centuries. Pliny the Elder described it in the first century CE:

> It is a remarkable circumstance, that the barbarous nations which subsist on milk have been for so many ages either ignorant of the merits of cheese, or else have totally disregarded it; and yet they understand how to thicken milk and form therefrom an acrid kind of milk with a pleasant flavour.[23]

Yoghurt production requires only milk, a bacterial culture and some warmth, but it can be manipulated into a vast number of products. It is a staple food in much of the world, but it is also sold in countries where it has not always been consumed. It was marketed first as a diet food; then – to make it more appealing to those who were not used to its tanginess – many varieties of sweetened yoghurts were developed. Since then, Westerners have been introduced to *lassi*, and recently so-called 'Greek' yoghurt, a thick version that is merely strained to rid it of excess water. Ironically, most yoghurt is not strained in Greece, although many varieties of strained yoghurt are made around the Eastern Mediterranean and South Asia. Examples include *labneh*, from several Arabic-speaking countries; Egyptian *zabadi*; Indian *chakka*; Iranian *mâst chekide*; Iraqi *laban*; and Turkish *kese yğurdu* and *süzme yoğurt*. Modern strained yoghurts are either cultured from milk that has first had some of its water removed by ultra-filtration, or excess water is extracted, after the fact, by filtration and/or centrifuging.

The Mongols' *aaruuls*, cheese curds, are dried in the sun. The Turkana peoples of Kenya do much the same, spreading the curds on sun-baked rocks or even cowhides. Bangladeshi *channa*, dried

Borden's evaporated milk, canned for the export market. Note that it is unsweetened, unlike condensed milk.

milk solids, are flavoured with sugar and sometimes cardamom. Reconstituted and cooked *channa* can be formed into balls or cut into cubes (or even dipped in chocolate). It is a popular street food. Foods prepared by people of lower castes are forbidden to observant Hindus; sweets and fried foods are exceptions to the rule, so are commonly available in public.

Pliny was surprised that 'the barbarous nations' were unfamiliar with cheeses, since Romans knew them well. Traditionally, cheese is made by curdling milk proteins with rennet obtained from the lining of animal stomachs. The process was probably discovered – by accident, in prehistoric times – when fresh milk was transported in such 'skins'. Pliny even classified the milk of various animals according to how much cheese could be produced from similar quantities of each, as well as which rennets were most efficacious: 'The rennet of the fawn, the hare, and the kid is the most esteemed, but the best of all is that of the dasypus [a kind of armadillo].'[24]

Cheeses can be made without rennet; in fact, all that is needed is an acid to curdle the milk. Lemon juice will do, as will any number of vegetable substances. Indian *paneer* is just such a cheese. Strict vegetarians shun cheese made with rennet, though Jews who keep kosher – oddly enough – don't consider rennet a meat product (which would violate Leviticus' rule against combining meat and dairy). Today, most rennet does not come from calves' stomachs, but is produced by special genetically modified bacteria that generate increased levels of the enzyme chymosin, which is rennet's active ingredient.

Traces of the oldest known cheeses were discovered at an archaeological dig in the Taklamakan Desert of northwestern China. Lumps of dessicated curds, dated to 1615 BCE, had been made using a mixture of yeast and a bacterial starter. Farmer cheese, pot cheese, quark and *fromage blanc* are modern strained versions. Cheeses begin as milk that may or may not be fermented with bacteria, moulds or yeast (or some mixture of these organisms) before being curdled. Fresh cheese curds, no matter how coagulated, are drained of excess whey, and subjected to many different processes that alter the final product. They may be pressed, cured, dried, smoked, inoculated with mould or bacteria, or any combination of the above. They may be rinsed with beer, wine or odoriferous slurries of bacteria. They can be wrapped in different materials, such as grape or chestnut leaves, crushed herbs or spices, paper, cloth, wax or plastic. The choice of wrapping determines the kinds of bacteria that modify the cheese curd; obviously, aerobic bacteria will not thrive in a cheese covered with impermeable wax or plastic.

Propionibacter shermanii, the bacteria responsible for the holes in Swiss-type cheeses, consume lactic acid produced by earlier fermentation, generating carbon dioxide that forms bubbles in the cheese paste. The milk for cheeses like Emmental and Jarlsberg is first fermented to create the acidic environment required by *P. shermanii*. It should be noted that recent research by the Swiss agricultural institute Agroscope suggests that the holes are not caused by *P. shermanii* – as proposed by William Clark, in 1917. They now believe that tiny bits of hay in the milk are responsible for the cheese's characteristic holes. This research has not yet been peer reviewed, or tested by others, at this time. It may be that hay particles merely provide nucleation sites where carbon dioxide bubbles could form.

Penicillium moulds, however, will not thrive in an acidic medium. So milk destined for blue- or green-veined cheeses (Roquefort and Gorgonzola), and white-bloomed cheeses (Brie and Camembert) is never cultured before curdling. *Brevibacterium linens*, an aerobic bacterium that requires air and a salty non-acidic environment to survive, yields smelly washed-rind cheeses such as Époisses and Limburger that develop a characteristic brownish-reddish surface.

Perhaps the most unusual cheeses are those that depend upon insects to develop their characteristic aromas, flavours and textures. The larvae or maggots of certain cheese flies (*Piophila casei*), while digesting the cheese, release enzymes that break down the proteins and fats, and create a taste sensation that encourages cheese-lovers to overlook the wriggling creatures on their plates. The maggots may, or may not, be consumed with the same gusto. Odd as it may seem to those who are repulsed by the idea of live insects in their food, maggot-infested cheeses are made in many places, including Abruzzo (*marcetto*); Calabria (*casu du quagghiu*); Corsica (*casgiu merzu*); Friuli Venezia Giulia (*saltarello*); Liguria (*gorgonzola co-i grilli*); Lombardy (*formai nis*); Sardinia (*casu marzu* or *casu fràzigu*); and Spain (*cabrales*). Less threatening is the lovely orange French cheese *mimolette*, which, unfortunately for American cheese-enthusiasts, was for some time banned from U.S. markets because of the presence of cheese mites (*Acarus siro*) in its cantaloupe-like rind. German *Milbenkäse* is actually named for the mites that create it (the name means 'mite cheese'), although these mites are a different species (*Tyrolichus casei* – the Latin name reflecting their region and favourite food) from the ones found on *mimolette*.

James Lewis Kraft patented the first canned cheese, a bland sterilized product originally called 'American Cheese', in 1916. He had been selling cheeses from a pushcart in Chicago, and was troubled by losses due to spoilage. It was during the golden age of canning, so it was only natural that he would turn to that technology.

> Sterilised emulsified canned cheese may be absolutely consistent and may keep forever, but a lot of folk feel that it is bland and – well, just ain't cheese. Kraft's timing however was perfect. One organisation that does not care a hoot about flavour but cares a lot of hoots about durability in food is the military. Six million pounds of his cheese ended up in ration packs during World War I.[25]

Kraft's 'American Cheese' was similar to, but not exactly the same as, the American cheese sold today. It at least was actually made of scraps of other cheeses (mostly cheddars and Colby). Today's version is legally required to be called 'cheese food', and is made from milk, milk protein concentrate, milkfat, whey, whey protein concentrate and – of course – salt.

For other dairy foodstuffs, Gail Borden was the first to produce canned milk products, and today condensed, evaporated and powdered milk are produced and consumed worldwide. These products have different characteristics that lend themselves to different uses. Powdered milk, obviously, has had all of its water removed. It requires no canning or refrigeration. Condensed and evaporated milks have had 60 per cent of their water removed. The primary difference between them is that condensed milk is sweetened with as much 45 per cent of sugar before having the water removed. This gives it a thick, slightly caramelized taste.

Brazilians capitalize on condensed milk's characteristics, and the fact that it comes in a can. They slowly heat it, in its slightly opened can, until it becomes a golden-brown semi-solid mass. This *dulce de leche* is then cooled, slipped out of its can and served as a kind of pudding.

Unlike in other countries, eggs are sold in the refrigerated dairy section of American markets. This seems odd, since mammals (other than a few monotremes, like the platypus and echidna) don't lay eggs – but there is a reason. In the U.S., eggs may be much older than a week, and refrigeration increases their shelf lives. While unrefrigerated eggs might disconcert American shoppers, there is little chance of spoilage if eggs are consumed within a week or so of being laid. American eggs, which might be older than a week, must comply with certain government guidelines:

The USDA requires producers to wash eggs with warm water at least 20°F warmer than the internal temperature of the eggs and at a minimum of 90°F. A detergent that won't impart any foreign odors to the eggs must also be used. After washing, the eggs must be rinsed with a warm

Dulce de Leche

1 can sweetened condensed milk,
any size, label removed

Punch two small holes in the top of the can (don't skip this step or you could have a very messy explosion). Place a piece of cloth, or small wire rack, on the bottom of a pot deep enough to hold the can. This will prevent annoying rattling noises while the can cooks. Place the can on top of the cloth or rack, punched end up, and fill the pot with water to between ½ and 1 inches (1.25– 2.5 cm) below the top of the can. Heat until it reaches a simmer, then adjust the temperature to hold it at that level for three to four hours, depending on how firm you want the *dulce de leche* to be. Check the water level periodically to make sure that it is neither too low or too high (too low could lead to scorching, too high and the water might get into the lid's holes). Finally, remove from heat and allow to cool. Open the can and serve.

Note: If cooked for the shorter time, the soft *dulce de leche* may have an uneven texture (the bottom is often firmer than the top) that can be easily whisked.

water spray containing a chemical sanitizer to remove any remaining bacteria.[26]

Once American eggs are washed, about 10 per cent of them are sealed in a thin coating of mineral oil. The practice is gradually being discontinued because modern egg production and distribution has eliminated the need for the long storage that used to make up for the fact that hens lay more eggs in the cooler months of the year.

Ironically, washing may actually cause them to spoil faster. If there is any moisture on the outside of an egg – as when condensation forms on cold eggs exposed to warm moist air – airborne bacteria can use it to pass through tiny pores in the shells of eggs that have had their protective cuticles removed by cleaning. Many countries, including all those in the EU, do not allow washed eggs to be sold, and eggs are not kept refridgerated there.

As we saw in the discussion of *Salmonella* poisoning, most U.S. farmers do not vaccinate their hens, so there is a very good chance that eggs arrive at stores already carrying some of the bacteria

Breaking eggs for pasteurization in Stepney, London, 1964.

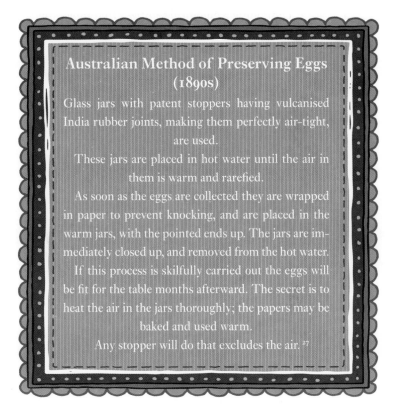

Australian Method of Preserving Eggs
(1890s)

Glass jars with patent stoppers having vulcanised India rubber joints, making them perfectly air-tight, are used.

These jars are placed in hot water until the air in them is warm and rarefied.

As soon as the eggs are collected they are wrapped in paper to prevent knocking, and are placed in the warm jars, with the pointed ends up. The jars are immediately closed up, and removed from the hot water.

If this process is skilfully carried out the eggs will be fit for the table months afterward. The secret is to heat the air in the jars thoroughly; the papers may be baked and used warm.

Any stopper will do that excludes the air. [27]

inside their shells. Refrigeration slows the growth of *Salmonella*, making the eggs safe for consumption up to three weeks after they are laid. Still, according to FDA data 'there are about 142,000 illnesses every year caused by consuming eggs contaminated by the most common strain of salmonella.'[28]

Before refrigeration was an option (and, presumably, before the rampant spread of *Salmonella*), innovators came up with a number of other techniques for extending the usable lives of eggs. A variation from China spawns the famous (or infamous) *pidan*, better known in the West as Thousand-year Eggs. These eggs – from chickens, ducks or quail – are slathered in a caustic slurry of ashes, clay, lime and salt. After being rolled in rice hulls,

Preserving with Lime (1910)

Dissolve in each gallon of water 12 ounces of quick-lime, 6 ounces of common salt, 1 drachm of soda, 0.5 drachm saltpeter, 0.5 drachm tartar, and 1.5 drachms of borax. The fluid is brought into a barrel and sufficient quicklime to cover the bottom is then poured in. Upon this is placed a layer of eggs, quicklime is again thrown in and so on until the barrel is filled so that the liquor stands about 10 inches deep over the last layer of eggs. The barrel is then covered with a cloth, upon which is scattered some lime.[29]

Preserving in Sodium Silicate (1916)

Dissolve sodium silicate in boiling water, to about the consistency of a syrup (or about 1 part of the silicate to 3 parts water). The eggs should be as fresh as possible, and must be thoroughly clean. They should be immersed in the solution in such manner that every part of each egg is covered with the liquid, then removed and let dry. If the solution is kept at or near the boiling temperature, the preservative effect is said to be much more certain and to last longer.[30]

they undergo many chemical reactions over the following several months (not 1,000 years!).

Fruits and Vegetables

Fruits are among the most often preserved foods. They tend to have short seasons of availability, large yields at harvest, high nutritional content and great taste appeal. Many of them are fermented, of course, but they are also canned, frozen and dehydrated. Dried fruits – apples, dates, figs, raisins and stone fruits – are also common. Chinese cooks use dried tangerine peel in several classic recipes. It is especially good in Chinese red-cooked meat dishes that are slowly braised in soy sauce, rice wine and five-spice powder.

Fruits and vegetables, being moist, are easily spoiled, so they have been subjected to many forms of preservation through-out (and, no doubt, before) recorded history. They have been dehydrated, salted, fermented, canned, frozen and bombarded

Dried tangerine peel is used as a flavouring in Chinese cooking. Packages of salted black beans often contain tangerine peel.

Dried apricots, their bright orange colour preserved with sulphur dioxide.

with radiation. Using modern dehydration methods, dried fruits from the tropics, where humidity might have prevented drying in the past – bananas, papayas and mangoes – are becoming increasingly familiar in more northern climes.

The Shakers, members of a utopian religious sect, among others, realized that there was a market for fruits well beyond their brief seasonal availability. This was long before high-speed transportation, refrigeration and low-atmosphere storage made it possible to have fresh fruit year-round. Preservation permitted

Imambayeldi, literally 'the Imam fainted'; these stuffed and jarred aubergines are a classic Turkish appetizer, although this particular jar comes from Armenia.

Vegetable preserves.

customers to have fruit that approached 'freshness', instead of the jellies, jams, fruit leathers and other dried varieties they had known for centuries. Bottling was the 'wave of the future' for farmers and orchardists.

The Ball Company, founded in 1880, published the first issue of their how-to book for home preservers, the *Blue Book*, less than 30 years later. Jars, of all sizes, lend themselves to fruit preservation. Even today, home preservers sometimes refer to these containers as 'fruit jars', regardless of their contents.

Fruits, whole or otherwise, can be kept in alcohol, such as peaches or cherries in brandy, or in syrup. Various conserves – *murabba* (India), or *varenye* (Belarus, Russia and Ukraine) – are whole fruits covered with unjelled syrup. They also appear in a wide range of thicker 'preserves': chutneys (spicy mixtures, usually accompanying meat or vegetable curries, though in Britain they are paired with cheese and cold meats); confits; butters (spiced purées, reduced to thick spreadable pastes); curds (smooth egg-based

Advertisement for
Libby's Tomato
Juice, 1952.

custards); jams (chopped or crushed fruits in pectin-thickened sugar gels); jellies (a clear version of jam using fruit juice); and spreads (like jam, but without added sugar).

Due to the high cost of fresh pineapples, for nearly a century many consumers were familiar only with the canned variety, which English and German consumers began to receive from Australia's Queensland Pineapple Company in 1892. Americans got theirs from James Dole, who began growing them in Wahiawa, Hawaii, in 1901. By 1903, within a year of his first harvest, he shipped almost 2,000 cases of canned pineapple to the mainland. Within two years, his production had increased over tenfold. Pineapples, once available only to the wealthy, had been democratized by Dole and the American Can Company's factory.[31]

Indians have two distinct categories of preserved vegetable and fruit condiments: chutneys and pickles. Chutneys (*chatnis*) tend to be sweet and somewhat spicy, and are based primarily on fruits. Pickles (*achars*) are intense; they are salty, sour, very spicy, often oil-based mixtures that feature vegetables or strong-tasting fruits, like lemons, limes or sour green mangoes. *Achars* often feature lots of chilli, mustard oil and asafoetida – a resin that, before it is cooked, is extremely foul-smelling (one of its kinder nicknames is 'devil's dung'), but adds a savoury leek-garlic scent after it is heated in fats or oils. This haughty description of *achars* was included in a letter received about 100 years ago:

Rough fruit chutney, a sweet and tangy companion to savoury dishes.

A Mode of Pickling Melons or
Cucumbers so as to Imitate Real Mangoes (1814)

Cut a square piece out of the sides of melons or cucumbers, and take out the seeds with a teaspoon. Put the fruit into very strong salt and water for a week, stirring them well two or three times a day. Then place them in a pan, on a good quantity of vine (or cabbage) leaves, and cover them over with as many more. Beat fine a little roche alum, put it into the salt and water, out of which the melons have been taken, pour it over them and set them on a very slow fire for four or five hours or till they get a good green.

Take them out, drain them in a hair sieve, and when cold, fill into them horseradish, mustard seed, garlic, and pepper corns. If the fruit be cucumbers, put a few slices of cucumbers in the center of the mixed stuffing. Sew on with thread the pieces taken out, and to every gallon of vinegar for covering and preserving them add an ounce each of mace and cloves; two ounces each of allspice, sliced ginger root and long and black pepper; two ounces of garlic; a large stick of horseradish; and three ounces of mustard seed tied up in a bag.

Boil this well together for a few minutes only; and pouring it on the pickles, close up the jar air-tight. The confinement of the mustard seed in a bag, is a very good method to adopt on other occasions.[32]

The method of pickling in oil is of all others in most request with the common people, who eat the greasy substance as a relish to their bread and dhall. The mustard-oil used in the preparation of this dainty is often preferred to ghee in curries.[33]

The 'common people' knew a good thing when they tasted it – the pickles sold by the *acharwallas* were more loaded with flavour than the more 'civilized' pickles Mrs Ali preferred:

The better sort of people prefer water pickle, which is made in most families during the hot and dry weather by a simple method; exposure to the sun being the chemical process to the parboiled carrots, turnips, radishes, &c., immersed in boiling water, with red pepper, green ginger, mustard-seed, and garlic. The flavour of this water pickle is superior to any other acid, and possesses the property of purifying the blood.[34]

Pickled baby aubergines.

India has plenty of mangoes, and a climate that desperately calls for imaginative forms of preservation. When we look at old cookbooks from Britain and America, we also find recipes for 'mangoes', which seems odd, since tropical mangoes are relatively recent additions to these nations' kitchens. It turns out that cooks in the Northern Hemisphere were imaginative too. Recipes for pickled faux 'mangoes' might even be made with bell peppers (capsicums) – a far cry from the spicy pickles made from real mangoes in Hawaii, India, Mauritius, the Philippines and Vietnam.

An early, and much appreciated, accidental discovery was finding that the sugar-rich juices of fruits make ideal breeding environments for airborne yeasts. We can only imagine the joy of the first person to try some spoiled grape juice, but we do know that it happened a long time ago, since residues of grape wine have been found in Iranian pots, left unwashed, from around 5400 BCE. Other alcoholic beverages are even older; a fragment of a Chinese pot has revealed traces of a beer-like brew made 11,000 years ago.[35]

Never content to leave a good thing alone, people began tinkering with wine early on. The Romans boiled it down to syrup, *caroenum*, for use in cooking. They flavoured wine with herbs, honey and spices to make *conditum*, while the Greeks preferred (and still prefer) to use tree resins that might also have functioned as a preservative. Modern *retsina* is descended from ancient wines that were shipped in *amphorae* sealed with sticky sap from pine trees. The Chinese discovered, by the twelfth century, that distillation increased the potency of their potables. They may have been distilling 1,000 years earlier, in the Han Dynasty, but we do not know if they were making alcohol. High-powered distilled beverages were produced in Italy during the thirteenth century.

A simpler method of increasing the alcohol content, sometimes called a 'Mongolian Still', required no special equipment – just some cooperative weather. Water freezes at a higher temperature than alcohol, so if a barrel is left to freeze, the ice can be removed, leaving a liquid with a higher alcohol content. Each time

Hand-coloured woodcut of an early still, in *Liber de arte distillandi de compositis* by Hieronymus Brunschwig (1512).

the liquid is frozen, the ratio of alcohol in the liquid increases, so it has a lower freezing point. A series of refreezings, each time at a lower temperature, gradually raises the alcohol content (proof). The fermented juice of apples (hard cider) can be turned into applejack via fractional freezing, to achieve a maximum of 40 per cent alcohol (80 proof). Unfortunately, freeze distillation also concentrates poisonous methanol – so stronger applejacks are made using modern fractional distillation, which is the method used for whisky, vodka and brandy (fractional distillation exploits the different boiling points of ethanol and methanol). German *Eisbocks* are made from bock beers by freezing, but don't reach dangerous concentrations of undesirable alcohols; they are bottled at 12 per cent alcohol. North American ice beers are actually brewed at sub-freezing temperatures, allowing ice to be removed during brewing. Well-known examples include Bud Ice, Maximum Ice, Molson Ice and Natural Ice, with alcohol contents ranging from 5.5 per cent to 7.1 per cent.

Ripe garden tomatoes, marinated in vinegar, with dill and bay leaves.

Vegetables occupy a large percentage of our larders. Even though today's markets are filled with frozen and fresh vegetables from all over the world, we still seem to prefer certain vegetables to arrive in cans. A host of tomato products – whole, crushed, stewed or puréed as paste, as well as sauce, soups and ketchup – are canned or bottled products. Far more tomatoes are consumed in preserved form than fresh.

Vegetables were among the first foods canned. Those that were only available for very short periods each year were especially prized. Garden peas, before canning, were uncommon on tables – except in their dried form. Soon corn, beets, green beans, carrots, potatoes and even spinach found their way

Peas were among the earliest canned vegetables. The factory that made this can was situated to take advantage of shipping via Lake Erie and by rail.

into cans (Popeye not withstanding, spinach is one of the least successful canned vegetables). Tomatoes were especially suited to canning. They are fragile and perishable but their high acidity makes them practically immune to bacterial spoilage.

The Shakers had made a name for themselves by selling high-quality seeds and plain, yet elegant, home furnishings. They were among the earliest adopters of canning technology.

> Canning gives the American family – especially in cities and factory towns – a kitchen garden where all good things grow, and where it is always harvest time . . . A regular Arabian Nights garden, where raspberries, apricots, olives and pineapples are always ripe, grow side by side with peas, pumpkins, spinach; a garden with baked beans, vines and spaghetti bushes, and sauerkraut beds,

HEINZ BAKED BEANS

WITH TOMATO SAUCE.

The beans are actually BAKED, not boiled. The quantity for each can is weighed to insure uniform proportion of beans and sauce. No such flavor found in any other.

SWEET PICKLES,

TOMATO KETCHUP,   TOMATO SOUP,

INDIA RELISH,   PRESERVES,

CELERY SALAD,   TOMATO CHUTNEY,

MUSTARD DRESSING.

Altogether **57** Varieties of
Pure Food **57** Products,

Which are distributed everywhere through our Branch Houses.

PRINCIPAL PLANT,—PITTSBURGH, U.S.A.

Heinz baked beans with tomato sauce trade card. The '57' didn't actually refer to the number of products the company offered; Henry J. Heinz just liked the sound of the number!

and great cauldrons of hot soups, and through it running a branch of the ocean in which one can catch salmon, lobsters, crabs and shrimp, and dig oysters and clams.[36]

For a long time, the Culinary Institute of America refused to teach its student chefs how to make tomato soup. They reasoned that anyone who might order a bowl of the iconic soup had already

Campbell's condensed soup can.

Canned Heinz Company products in the window of the store Tousignant & Frère, Montreal.

been conditioned to prefer the one made by Campbell's. Anything else, no matter how fresh, would be perceived as being somehow 'wrong'. Similarly, baked beans can be made, from scratch, with dried haricot beans (also known as pea or navy beans). In practice, however, most come out of cans produced by the popular brands Campbell's, Heinz, Bush's or B&M. Generations of children have grown up eating these brands, and are unlikely to return to the old-fashioned (and time-consuming) preparations of the past.

Fungi, or mushrooms, pop up briefly each year, but can add a depth of flavour to dishes year-round – if they can be preserved. Fortunately, several methods work well. We need not limit ourselves to the little tins we find on our grocer's shelves, such as common button mushrooms, the more interesting Chinese straw mushrooms and Japanese *enoki* mushrooms. Drying is a better way to preserve fungi: their flavours deepen in the process. Dried mushrooms are staples in Europe, where boletes, porcini, chanterelles and morels are hunted and saved for use long after their short seasons have passed. The Chinese, who are masters of food preservation (especially of foods that are dense with the 'fifth taste', umami), have been drying mushrooms for centuries. No Chinese market would be without bins – or cellophane bags – of dried shiitakes, tree ears and cloud ears. Dried mushrooms need to be rehydrated before they can be used in cooking. The hot water used for this purpose should never be discarded, as it is loaded with the mushroom flavour and can be added to sauces, or reduced in the same pan in which the mushrooms are cooked, so that it can be reabsorbed. Dried mushrooms can also be ground to a powder and added directly to dishes as they cook.

Perhaps the most famous fungal delicacy, and the most expensive, is the truffle. These lumpy, misshapen subterranean mushrooms, of the genus *Tuber*, are usually consumed fresh, but their heady aroma can be extracted and saved in the form of truffle-scented salt, oils and even vodka. However, whenever serious money is involved (one especially large truffle sold for u.s. $330,000 (£165,000)) at an auction in 2007, unscrupulous individuals notice.

To Make the Mushroom Powder (1739)

Take a peck of Mushrooms, wash and rub them clean with a flannel rag, cutting out all the worms; but do not peel off the skins: put to them sixteen blades of mace, forty cloves, six bay-leaves, twice as much beaten pepper as will lie on a half crown; a good handful of salt, a dozen onions, a piece of butter as big as an egg, and half a pint of vinegar: stew these as fast as you can; keep the liquor for use, and dry the Mushrooms first on a broad pan in the oven; afterwards put them on sieves, till they are dry enough to pound all together into powder. This quantity usually makes half a pound.[37]

To Pickle Mushrooms (1604)

Take your Buttons, clean them with a spunge & put them in cold water as you clean them, then put them dry in a stewpan & shake a handful of salt over them, then stew them in their own liquor till they are a little tender; then strain them from the liquor & put them upon a cloath to dry till they are quite cold. Make your Pickle before you do your Mushrooms, that it may be quite cold before you put them in. The Pickle must be made with White-Wine, White-Pepper, quarter'd Nutmeg, a Blade of Mace, & a Race of ginger.[38]

Another Sort of Mushroom-Powder (1739)

Take the large Mushrooms, wash them clean from grit cut off the stalks, but do not peel or gill them; so put them into a kettle over the fire, but no water; put a good quantity of spice of all sorts, two onions stuck with cloves, a handful of salt, some beaten pepper, and a quarter of a pound of butter; let all these stew, till the liquor is dried up in them; then take them out, and lay them on sieves to dry, till they will beat to powder; press the powder hard down in a pot, and keep it for use, what quantity you please at a time in sauce.[39]

Dried black
fungus (Jew's ear
mushroom).

A truffle by any other name may smell as sweet, but what if that name is 2,4-dithiapentane? All across the country, in restaurants great and small, the 'truffle' flavor advertised on menus is increasingly being supplied by truffle oil. What those menus don't say is that, unlike real truffles, the aroma of truffle oil is not born in the earth. Most commercial truffle oils are concocted by mixing olive oil with one or more compounds like 2,4-dithiapentane (the most prominent of the hundreds of aromatic molecules that make the flavor of white truffles so exciting) that have been created in a laboratory.[40]

Starches

Starches, especially preserved starches, made civilization possible. Even after millennia, with modern nutritionists advising us to cut back on them, starchy foods – such as pasta, couscous, rice and rice noodles, cornmeal, hominy, masa, arrowroot and tapioca – coddle us as 'comfort food'; their blandness makes them a perfect foil for spicy dishes, and they are both inexpensive and filling. Potatoes, being high in moisture, are one of the few starches that do not preserve easily (except in high-altitude, arid places). However, spuds still manage to find their way into cans, freezer bags, crisp (chip) packets and boxes of dehydrated mashed potatoes.

Unidentified dried mushrooms in a Chinese market.

Beverages

It is hard to believe that there was a time when Western cultures did not indulge regularly in caffeinated drinks, but, before the sixteenth century, they had none. The Age of Exploration connected Europe with the places where plants that produce caffeine grow. Each of the following stimulating beverages requires processing, both to preserve and develop their flavours.

Chocolate was used as a beverage long before it was sweetened and converted into a sweet treat. Cacao's flavour is merely bitter before undergoing two fermentations. First the loosely packed beans are inoculated with *acetobacilli* (provided by ever-present fruit flies) which liquefies the pulp surrounding the seeds, creating a slightly sour flavour. Acetic acid and the heat of the fermentation kills the seeds, preventing germination, and chemical changes involving yeasts and *lactobacilli* develop more complex flavours. At this point, they can be ground and whipped into a frothy drink – as was done by the Aztecs – or further processed into our familiar cocoa powder.

Tea is native to the Asian subcontinent, and did not find its way to Europe until the seventeenth century, although the Chinese had been brewing it for over 3,500 years. Samuel Pepys wrote about his first taste of the new phenomenon on 25 September 1660: 'I did send for a cup of tee, (a China drink) of which I had never had drunk before.' It was probably a Chinese black tea, the leaves of which were fermented before being dried. Japanese green teas (dried, but unfermented) and smoked teas – like *lapsang souchong* – arrived somewhat later. All of the different styles of tea are made from the same plant, but differ in methods of picking, drying, oxidizing, fermenting, steaming, smoking and heating to create completely different colours, aromas, flavours and degrees of astringency.

Coffee was originally discovered growing in Ethiopia, so long ago that its discovery is wrapped in myth and legend. It was first mentioned in Arabic writings from the tenth century but was probably familiar long before that. After fermentation coffee beans are dried for storage and shipping. Perhaps the most unusual form of coffee fermentation occurs in the gut of the Asian palm civet (*Paradoxurus hermaphroditus*). After eating the coffee cherries, the animal excretes the 'cleaned' beans, which are collected and sold as a luxury coffee called *kopi luwak*.

Whichever method frees coffee of its pulpy exterior, loose green beans are not immediately roasted. The reason is that heating releases oils that oxidize, producing an unpleasant rancid taste. They were only shipped in roasted form, in the past, because roasted beans cannot germinate (in an attempt to protect the Arab traders' monopoly). Today's ready-roasted beans are sold under vacuum in bags or cans to discourage rancidity.

South Americans had sources of caffeine or caffeine-like compounds long before the Old World brought them coffee and tea. Well-to-do Aztecs had *chocolatl*, and Incas had coca leaves, of course, but the natives of what is now Argentina had *maté* (*Ilex paraguariensis*), and the inhabitants of the huge Amazon basin had *guaraná* (*Paullinia cupana*). The seeds of *guaraná* are roasted, ground and brewed like coffee, but have three times the caffeine content of coffee. They also contain tea's theophylline and cacao's theobromine. *Guaraná* energizes South American soft drinks that have made their way into the U.S., especially around college campuses, where it is consumed by students trying to power their way through all-nighters.

At the opposite of the stimulant spectrum are the herbal teas. Technically, they are *tisanes*, brews of dessicated flowers and herbs that are intended to smooth 'the ravell'd sleeve of care', as Shakespeare terms the worried mind, by not interfering with the healing powers of sleep. Linden tea, however, made from the dried flowers of *Tilia cordata*, produced the insomnia that liberated *les temps perdu* from Proust's madeleine.

Desserts

'Pudding', in England, is roughly equivalent to the American 'dessert'. American puddings are usually smooth, starch-thickened products, ironically similar to *crème anglaise*. The earliest American puddings had more texture, even though they were also based on starch. Bread pudding, a moister version of *pain perdu*, makes economical use of leftover stale bread; creamy rice pudding turns leftover cooked rice into dessert; while Indian pudding (recipes for which appeared in Amelia Simmons's cookbook, the first written by an American) was based on cornmeal. Most Americans today are more familiar with puddings that come in little cardboard boxes – many of which do not even require cooking, because they are thickened by specially modified food starches that gel at low temperatures. Instant gelatine desserts arrive in similar boxes. Desserts made of gelatine have been served since the fifteenth century, but they were very labour-intensive. Bones, connective tissues and hides had to be boiled to extract collagen, and then meticulously clarified. Peter Cooper, who constructed the first steam engine

Cover of a promotional booklet of recipes, 1924.

No matter where
you live you get this
perfect package of
JELL-O at
all times of the year

built in the United States, also invented the first powdered gelatine in 1845. Charles B. Knox patented a flavoured version in 1890, and then sold the patent to Pearle Bixby Wait, who came up with a fruit flavoured product in 1897. Wait's wife called it Jell-O. Unable to market the product themselves, they sold its name and patent, two years later, to Frank Woodward's Genesee Pure Food Company, allegedly for $450. By 1906 the company was selling over $1 million worth of the little boxes per year.

FIVE

Geography

As the saying goes, 'Location, location, location'. Geography makes a huge difference to our eating habits. Localized variations in natural resources, climate, language and religion help to distinguish the ways in which one locale preserves its foods from those of other places – even those of their neighbours. When one culinary culture is isolated from others, it tends to develop very distinctive cuisines based entirely on its own resources and culture. Conversely, when a culture has had a lot of contact with other cultures (through conquest, trade and so on), it becomes more cosmopolitan, and therefore less distinctive.

Until relatively recently Italy was composed of warring city-states that even had dialects that were largely incomprehensible to their neighbours. As a result, Florentines consider Sienese dishes to be 'foreign food', and Rome's residents regard the cuisine of the Neapolitans in the same way. An outsider might see that *cacciatore* and *cacciatorini* (small dried sausages, ideally sized for a hunter to carry in his pocket) can be found in seven provinces, and suspect that they are all the same. They are not; only the names and usage are similar.

Non-Italians tend to think that everyone in Italy has always eaten dried pasta slathered in sauce made from canned tomatoes. The truth is that they had never even seen a tomato before the New World was discovered, and dried pasta didn't become an inexpensive commodity until industrialized versions appeared in the nineteenth century. Different regions of Italy that have had extensive contact with other cultures have cuisines that evolved very differently from those of the more isolated locales. Once occupied by the Saracens, Sicilians today still use more cinnamon in their cooking than anywhere else in Italy. Furthermore, the food of Friuli-Venezia Giulia in northeastern Italy hardly seems 'Italian', due to its cooler climate and close contact with the nearby Germanic and Slavic peoples with whom the region shares a border.

Italy, of course, is not the only example. A recent study found that geographic distance was the leading influence on differences between Chinese regional cuisines.[1] Moreover, the Chinese have, for centuries, had major contact with other civilizations throughout South and Southeast Asia, and their styles of fermented and dried ingredients have been adopted, and adapted, almost everywhere they have travelled.

India, occupying a central position along ancient spice routes, has spread its culinary influence in all directions. Curries went east into Burma, China and Thailand. *Achars*, salted and fermented pickles, travelled east from Persia to India, where they achieved iconic status. They also journeyed eastward to Malaysia, where they were known as *atsjaar*. They went to the Eastern Mediterranean, where the seeds of the turpentine tree (*Pistacia terebinthus*), a source of the resin that flavoured and preserved some of the oldest wines ever found – at a 3,600-year-old site at Kabri, Israel – are pickled in vinegar and salt, and are still called *atsjaar*.[2] They also continued their westward migration as far as the Carolina coast of the U.S.:

> Harriet Pinckney Horry recorded a receipt '*Ats Jaar*' in her cookery manuscript dated 1770. It is significant that forms of the Persian/Indian name *achar* seem to have been nearly peculiar to the Low Country insofar as English or American cookery is concerned; that is, with one

exception . . . a receipt for *Atx Jar Pickle*, surely borrowed from Carolina sources . . . Hannah Glasse had given a similar receipt in *The Art of Cookery* . . . under the name *India Pickle*.[3]

In this case, the name for a salty pickle travelled more than halfway around the globe – even though the ingredients and techniques used for making the pickles did not.

Climate certainly affects the kinds of foods that people choose to preserve. Cool climates favour the growth of plants like mustard and horseradish, while warmer climates are associated with a different set of hot spices, such as chillies, black and long pepper, cubebs, Guinea pepper, ginger, cinnamon and Sichuan pepper. Before extensive trade routes were established, cooks would have used what was locally available. Today, it is hard to imagine the cuisines of India, Korea, Sichuan and Thailand before they had chillies. Obviously the people had a taste for hot spices, but their dishes would have had very different flavours before the sixteenth century.

Europeans were introduced to pepper as a result of Alexander the Great's incursions into India 2,500 years ago. The ancient Romans consumed vast amounts of pepper – both black and long species, as well as cubebs – but after the empire collapsed, the trade routes fell into disuse. The Crusades re-introduced Europeans to the joys of spices, which eventually led to the Age of Exploration. The search for one set of exotic ingredients led to the discovery of a host of new ones: chillies, chocolate and vanilla. It also brought new vegetables to the Old World – such as corn, peppers and tomatoes – that were to feature largely in their preserved foods.

Climate also determined the forms of preservation chosen. Arid climates fostered drying techniques. Pre-Columbian natives of the Andes made dried ribbons of llama meat called *ch'arki* – what we now call jerky (today, their descendants use beef, or horse as well). Egyptians dry a jerky-like product, *kavurmeh*, then protect it from air with a thick covering of ghee. Similar strips of beef or lamb are marinated in a Moroccan mixture of ground coriander and cumin seeds, garlic, salt and olive oil. After these are dried in the sun, they receive a thick coating of melted fat. Both African variations on French confit can keep, unrefrigerated, for as long as two years.

Sub-Saharan Africa is hot and humid, and often doesn't have easy access to salt, so drying, combined with smoking, has long been the preservation method of choice. The Bight of Benin, in the Gulf of Guinea, is rich in shellfish, and smoked shrimp are produced there. Fish and molluscs preserved in this way provide protein and umami-rich flavouring to otherwise bland, starchy (rice and millet) diets. The northern, more arid parts of Africa do have salt, so salted seafood is common. Egyptians make *fasikh* (or *fassekh*) from mullet or other small fish. Pungent Senegalese dried fish season dishes throughout the region.

Stockfish, from the North Atlantic, became a staple item on the western coast of Africa during the days of slavery in the Americas. That 'peculiar institution' of the American south led to some unexpected culinary traditions. The African taste for

> Smoked and dried fish (and other seafood like shellfish) supplied flavoring as well as protein, too . . . eventually smoked, salted pork replaced the smoked, salted fish in the diets of Africans brought as slaves to the southern United States.[4]

Slow-cooked greens, seasoned with smoky salted fish, are a staple in Africa – and similar pork products serve the same purpose in American soul food.

Keeping Things Moving

The standard jar of ancient Greece and Rome. These large ceramic jugs were used for shipping grain, *garum*, honey, olive oil and wine. The standard size held 39 litres (41 qts). The pointed bottom served two purposes: it allowed the jugs to be lowered into the holds of ships (stabilized in a bed of sand); and consolidated any sediment in their contents.

Preserved foods have been both the goal of, and the medium of exchange for, much of long-distance trade in history. We have already seen the interconnectedness of salt cod and sugar. And we know that the Age of Exploration came to pass as a result of attempts to bypass Islamic spice merchants. Arab merchants were protected from European competition because, after the fall of Constantinople in 1453, travel through the Middle East was blocked. Essentially, Europeans had to replace the caravans of the Silk Road with caravels on the high seas. In the process, they also replaced the Islamic monopoly with several Christian ones.

Even before attempts to bypass the monopoly of the spice traders, efforts had been made to dominate the transport of preserved foods and the materials needed for their preservation. The Hanseatic League was based on earlier guilds, but operated much like one of today's cartels. A group of several Germanic towns controlled all of the trade, including the all-important herring fishery, along the coasts of the North Sea and the Baltic, from Estonia to Brussels, for 400 years, beginning in the thirteenth century. One of the Hansa towns, Lüneberg, had salt works that have been in operation for some 800 years. Brine from Lüneberg's salt springs was evaporated in large pans (the cool climate did not permit the kind of open salt works found in the Mediterranean). Lüneberg's salt was more energy- and labour-intensive than open-air salt works, but its cost was justified because foods didn't dry very quickly in the cool northern air. The salt that prevented food spoilage was as critical to their economy as petroleum is to ours.

Further north, salt was even more expensive, so Swedes employed different strategies for food preservation, some of which are still in use today. *Surströmming* is lightly salted herring that undergoes additional fermentation which creates, along with tangy lactic and acetic acids, several other compounds. Many of the latter are off-putting to those unaccustomed to the food: butyric acid reeks of rancid butter; propionic acid has a pungent underarm aroma; and enough hydrogen sulphide gas makes cans bulge with the stench of rotten eggs. Clearly, they are not easily acquired tastes. Wolfgang Fassbender, a German food critic, said: 'The largest challenge in eating surströmming is to put off vomiting until *after* the first bite, instead of before.'[5]

Norwegian ratfisk (or *rakfisk*), similar to Swedish *surströmming* in its ability to make non-Nordic diners eschew all fish from their diets, is made by fermenting freshwater salmonids (chars and trout) in brine for up to three months. It is lightly pressed, discarding the sort of liquid that ancient Romans and modern Southeast Asians would treat as a condiment. Icelandic decomposed shark, *hákarl* – redolent of ammonia – is fermented (rotted, actually). Scandinavians, it seems, appear to have a well-developed tolerance for foul-smelling seafood.

Refinements to long-distance marine navigation (such as the improved Portuguese mariner's astrolabe, the Davis Quadrant and the English Quadrant – devices that made it possible to calculate one's latitude at sea) created competition for the Hanseatic League. Portuguese, British and Dutch fleets established routes to the Spice Islands and other exotic locales the Hanseatic League could never have imagined. Long-distance shipping led to the creation of all-new cartels, with corporations such as the Dutch East India Company, and several British corporations (the Royal African Company, the Honourable East India Company, the Levant Company), establishing themselves. Trade with tropical places not only lowered the price of spices, but introduced a host of new condiments and seasonings – the preserved foods of the East – to European kitchens.

Trade also led to the creation of some new European preserved foodstuffs. Long voyages required reliable supplies that could endure long exposure to hot and humid conditions. Hardtack, or sea biscuit, was a twice-baked slab of starch – virtually inedible on its own, but somewhat better if rehydrated and combined with salted pork or beef. To help wash it down, beer was safer than casks of questionable water. However, beer was apt to spoil on the long voyages, so the recipe was altered to preserve it. Increasing its alcohol content and adding more hops worked. The new-and-improved brew was called India Pale Ale (IPA).

Around the middle of the eighteenth century, better means of land transport became necessary. Horses and mules could not keep up with the demands for fuel and raw materials created by the Industrial Revolution. Over 4,000 miles of canals were excavated in England alone between 1759 and 1840. The French had already built a canal connecting the Atlantic coast, near Bordeaux, with the Mediterranean in Provence. In the U.S. in 1825 the Erie Canal was opened, connecting the Great Lakes to the Atlantic via the Hudson River. One of the immediate effects of this canal was the possibility of international trade between upstate New York farmers and customers on the other side of the ocean. Soon these rural farmers were shipping more cheddar cheese from New York's Herkimer County than was being produced in Somerset, England. The Erie, and a network of other canals, made it possible for Chicago to become the central meatpacker for the entire United States.

While canals could carry huge volumes of goods inexpensively, they had one serious limitation. They froze in winter. However, a solution was steaming over the horizon: railways. Within just a few decades, the age of canals was over, and trains began to transform the landscape. Many of the tracks were laid along the same routes as the canals, since they had already been cleared, and were relatively level for most of their routes. That meant that industries that had been built to make use of the canals did not have to relocate. One of those factories – for the H. J. Heinz Company, in Pittsburgh, Pennsylvania – was ideally situated to take advantage of navigation on three rivers, the Pennsylvania Canal and the new railroads. That meant it was in a perfect position to combine its safe and clean jarred foods with multiple means of transportation.

Heinz products are now ubiquitous all over the world (British visitors to the U.S. are sometimes surprised to learn that their favourite brand of baked beans is available in American stores). The popularity of Heinz pickles, sauces, soups and more in the UK are in part due to the efforts of another American: Harry Gordon Selfridge. His famous London store ran an ad in *The Times* in June 1939 calculated to create a demand for products like those of the H. J. Heinz Company:

> Many a time, having looked over the list of our American Groceries, we have felt for these departments a kinship with Brillat Savarin. Whether one considers the list carefully, or turns over its pages in desultory fashion, there is always something unusual, quite different in these biscuits and beans, fruits and preserves, syrups and vegetables from across the Atlantic. The very names are appetizing, opening up to the uninitiated a vista of future gastronomic delights. Corn Popper and Candied Yams, Blueberries in Syrup and Hominy, Melon Mangoes and Succotash – they seem to stir the imagination and titillate the least susceptible of salivary glands! And what of Brandied Peaches, or those tins of biscuits known as Koeppens Snappies, or Duff's Devil's Food Mixture, a packet flour famed in American kitchens?[6]

Other companies were also able to take immediate advantage of the new transportation systems. The meatpacker P. D. Armour used trains to deliver barrels of his salted meat to the Union armies during the Civil War. Armour had done very well with his modern mechanized processing of beef and pork, and the railroads were making distribution much more efficient, but he could do even better if there was a way to deliver meat without all those barrels and salt. Instead of shipping live animals to urban abattoirs, Midwest meatpackers – like Armour – wanted to sell *fresh* meat to the huge East Coast markets. Fresh meat had been shipped by rail by then, but could only survive the trip during the winter months. For year-round delivery, one of Armour's competitors, Gustavus Franklin Swift, hired the engineer Andrew Chase to improve on the experimental refrigerated railcars that others had tried. None had been successful before, because meat either rested on ice, causing it to become unappetizingly discoloured, or was suspended above the ice, causing the cars to sway uncontrollably when they went around bends and derailing the trains. Chase's idea was to pack the meat at the bottom of the cars (eliminating problems of trying to stablize the vehicles' centres of gravity) and placing a compartment of ice above the carcasses, allowing dense cold air to settle on them. Swift's plan for refrigerated cars allowed him to reach more distant markets for his dressed beef, but he had a difficult time finding a carrier that was interested in his idea. Eventually, the Grand Trunk Railway agreed to carry Swift's own cars. By 1881 he was in business as a shipper of dressed meat. For the first time, inexpensive fresh meat was available year-round, and barrels of salted meats became a thing of the past. The idea was so successful that between 1882 and 1886 the number of livestock cars travelling from Chicago to New York was reduced by one-quarter – but 26 times the number of refrigerated cars took the same route as at the beginning of that four-year period.

This development meant that all kinds of food could be kept fresh longer, which in turn created a demand for home refrigerators. Early home iceboxes began to be replaced by electric refrigerators in the 1920s. They had tiny freezer sections, but as the volume of frozen foods increased, freezer space had to grow along with them. By the 1950s, the advent of TV dinners and a wider range of other new frozen foods (such as fish sticks and Tater Tots) – as well as the diet-crazed years of the following decades, that featured Lean

Cuisine and similar frozen complete meals in a freezer tray – led to the development of free-standing, separate home freezers, as well as a frozen series of conveyances that went from factory, to trucks and railcars, to warehouses, to freezer displays in supermarkets.[7]

Places that have traditionally been without refrigeration, and require long travel times to visit, have often relied on canned meats. Hawaiians, for example, eat a lot of sushi (and other ethnic dishes) that have been modified to use Spam. Vienna Sausages are also popular there. Likewise, tinned Australian butter and Danish bacon are common on some of the smaller Caribbean islands.

Wars cause another form of isolation for which preserved foods are essential. The Hawaiians' taste for Spam can be traced to its introduction during the Second World War. Unlike most rationed foods in the U.S. and Britain, Spam was always available – 100 million pounds of it – whether one liked it or not. Rationing ended in America shortly after the war, but it did not completely end in Britain until 4 July 1954. Monty Python fans are probably running through the menu of their 'spam' routine, mentally, right now:

Egg and Spam
Egg, Bacon and Spam
Egg, Bacon, Sausage and Spam
Spam, Bacon, Sausage and Spam
Spam, Egg, Spam, Spam, Bacon and Spam
Spam, Spam, Spam, Egg and Spam
Spam, Spam, Spam, Spam, Spam, Spam, Baked Beans,
Spam, Spam, Spam and Spam
Lobster *Thermidor aux crevettes* with a mornay sauce,
    garnished with truffle pâté, brandy and a fried egg
    on top of Spam

Advertisement for Spam that ran in American magazines, early 1941.

That fried egg would have been the real treat – as a fresh egg could be enjoyed only once every other month during the war.

Powdered eggs, however, were always available (with a ration coupon, of course).

Why Certain Foods, and Their Preserving Methods, are Specific to Certain Locales

Europe is surrounded on three sides by water, so you would expect seafood to play a significant role in the diet there, but the Continent's seafood consumption is more convoluted than that.

Religion exerts a tremendous influence on cuisine. For a large part of Europe's history, the Roman Catholic Church has been the primary religion. The church calendar contains many meatless days (various saint's days, Lent and meatless Fridays). Contrary to popular 'fakelore', fish-on-Friday was not intended as a means to prop up a lagging fishing industry. Instead, the sacrifice of eschewing meat was meant to mirror Christ's Good Friday sacrifice. To supply all that seafood, in a period that lacked refrigeration, huge fleets of ships fished for herring (which was salted and smoked), and later for cod. Salted and dried cod could travel long distances overland, and later be reconstituted into something resembling fresh fish.

It is a curious fact that religious dogma tends to have more rules about prohibited foods than required ones. Vegetarianism is a principle of several religions, although many vegetarians shun meat for other reasons. Today's grocers, even in places where there are not large numbers of devout Jains, Buddhists and Hindus among their clientele, provide surrogate meat products such as faux sausages, bacon and turkey (with droll brand names like 'Fakin' Bacon', 'Not Dogs', 'Soyrizo' and 'Tofurkey'), which are produced in factories, and composed of soya protein, gluten and a host of other processed substances – such as soybean oil, tapioca starch and yeast extracts – all in an attempt to simulate the carnivore's dining experience.

Countries with large Buddhist populations have more varied (and more aesthetically pleasing) vegetarian cuisines. Over the last 2,000 years, Chinese cooks have used tofu in a vast number of dishes incorporating 'the meat without a bone'. That bland ingredient is typically rendered more appealing through the addition of salty, savoury or spicy condiments based on other (often fermented) soya products. By freezing, drying and/or frying tofu, a wide range of meat-like textures can be obtained. For example, dried bean-curd skin, an elastic protein-rich substance that forms during the coagulation of soya milk into tofu, is softened in water, then layered with spices, soy sauce and sesame oil, and pressed to make 'Buddhist Ham'.

Speaking of ham, everyone knows that pork is forbidden to Jews and Muslims. Both religions go into considerable detail about how 'unclean' pigs are. Why are these two religions the only ones that anathematize heavenly hams and succulent sausages of swine? There are two reasons, and neither is quite as divinely inspired as we might think. First, pigs cannot sweat, so they require shade and plenty of moisture on the outside of their bodies to cool them. If that water is provided to pigs kept in a sty (a small enclosed area), it is soon churned into a cooling (if odoriferous) bath of mud and excrement. The birthplace of Judaism and Islam does not have enough shade and water to share with pigs. Secondly, pigs, like us, are omnivores. They consume anything, including things that we like to eat, while cows, goats and sheep prefer to eat the plants that we do not. Herbivores turn useless foliage into desirable protein (both as meat and milk – or, as with some African pastoralists, blood). Pigs compete with us for limited food resources, don't produce much usable milk and provide neither fibres (wool or fur) nor 'horsepower'. This reality makes them a poor economic choice as a farm animal in the Middle East. The food traditions of Judaism and Islam were formulated in exactly the kind of place where pig-farming is impractical.[8]

Since the objections to pork are both economic and religious, one cannot expect to find pork sausages, bacon or ham in such an inhospitable environment. Sausages, there, are made of other meats (mostly lamb). Consider the fact that the country with the largest Muslim population, Indonesia, is tropically moist, and has an ideal climate for raising pigs. It is also the only Islamic country that enjoys pork dishes, like *babi ketjap* – slices of pork slowly simmered in thick sweet soy sauce and tangy tamarind paste.

Large populations relocate for many reasons: war, persecution and economic pressures. As a result, localized enclaves of unexpected ethnicities can be found scattered around the globe. This explains why one can find garlicky Portuguese sausages (*linguiça* and *choriço*) in small villages on the New England coast, or a market for odoriferous fermented fish pastes in South America: Javanese immigrants brought along their taste for the stuff when they moved to Suriname. North African spice merchants are commonly found on market days in rural France. West Indian curried goat is sold in London. Currywurst – a hot dog slathered with a mixture of ketchup and curry powder – is among the most popular street foods in Berlin. People are always

---

Florence Artificial Olives (1827)

Take young chestnuts or almonds; pick them of a handsome size and shape; make a lye of wood ashes sufficiently strong to bear an egg; have enough of this lye to cover the walnuts; pour it over hot, and cover them very well up; leave them from fourteen to twenty days; put them into a strong brine of salt and water, and leave them about the same time. Bottle them in this liquor for sale and use; but those that would have them superlatively good, must bottle them in equal quantities of Seville orange-juice and oil.[9]

Curious Secret of Making Artificial Olives, so as to Resemble in Taste and Appearance the Real Olive (1818)

Having procured, as a substitute for olives, some of the smallest green walnuts before there is any appearance of a shell, make a lie of wood ashes sufficiently strong to be capable of bearing an egg, boil enough of this lie to cover the walnuts, pour it hot over them, stop the vessel up close, and let them stand thus for at least two or three weeks, after which put them into a strong brine of salt and water, keep them so covered a fortnight, and then bottle them in the same liquor for use.[10]

moving, and they take their tastes with them. They also learn to incorporate ingredients and techniques they encounter in their new country, and all the places in between. When they cannot perfectly recreate the foods they love, they make substitutions.

Thomas Jefferson spent a great deal of time in Europe (much of it in France as the U.S. ambassador). While there, he developed a taste for French wines, which he was able to import to his home in Virginia. He tried, several times, to grow olives at his plantation, Monticello, and other southern locations, but with little success. Ironically, American-grown olives do exist today, but they were not on U.S. soil in Jefferson's time: they only grow in California. That didn't stop cooks from trying to make their own ersatz olives.

Cooks in England (another place where *Olea europaea* does not grow well) also tried to concoct surrogate olives. Some 'olives' are olives in name only. They don't even pretend to

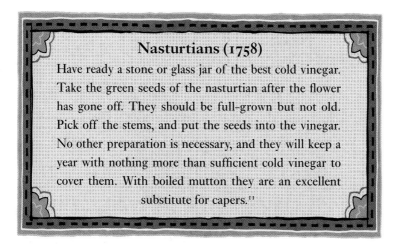

Nasturtians (1758)

Have ready a stone or glass jar of the best cold vinegar. Take the green seeds of the nasturtian after the flower has gone off. They should be full-grown but not old. Pick off the stems, and put the seeds into the vinegar. No other preparation is necessary, and they will keep a year with nothing more than sufficient cold vinegar to cover them. With boiled mutton they are an excellent substitute for capers.[11]

imitate olives. In fact, the only attributes they share with olives are their name and their shape. They acquired their name from Europeans who saw them for the first time, and it stuck, even among Asians who had no idea how an actual olive tasted. Chinese 'olives' are not olives at all, but the dried fruit of a subtropical evergreen tree (*Canarium* genus) that grows from Africa to the Philippines.

True capers (*Capparis spinosa*) grow on a spiny shrub that grows in the warm dry region around the Mediterranean. At least as early as the seventeenth century, cooks in more northern climes have been making *faux* capers – sometimes called 'Capuchin capers', from the French name for nasturtium, *capucine* (*Tropaeolum majus*).

Escabeche is not so much a dish as a class of dishes. It is a two-step process, in which food (originally fish) is first fried and then pickled. *Escabeche* was first made in Islamic kitchens in Persia. The Moors brought the method to the western Mediterranean coast (as far as the south of France and the Iberian peninsula). Variations are found all around the Mediterranean basin: Greek *savoro*, Algerian *scabetche* and Italian *scapece*. It later spread, via colonization, to Latin America and the Philippines. In Japan, *Nanbanzuke* ('southern barbarian pickle') is based on methods that were probably introduced by early Portuguese visitors.

Foods travelled in the other direction as well. The 'Columbian exchange' marked the introduction to Africa, Asia, Australia and Europe of New World ingredients (cacao, corn, beans, chillies, tomatoes and turkeys, among others).

Could we even imagine Italian food without tomatoes? They did not exist in Italy before the middle of the sixteenth century, and were not eaten for another 150 years – and even then, only because the Spanish had begun eating them. Over time, Italians developed their own varieties – thick-fleshed and deeply flavoured, like the San Marzanos that grow in the shadow of Vesuvius – that are ideal for making sauces. Yet such sauces did not even become an Italian staple until nineteenth-century canning technologies were adopted.

Almost every peasant cuisine in the world prides itself on a version of a dried legume paired with a starchy grain. Combinations of rice and beans, many of which would have been impossible before Columbus, are everywhere. *Mujaddara* is an

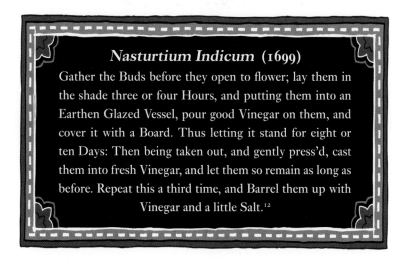

Nasturtium Indicum (1699)

Gather the Buds before they open to flower; lay them in the shade three or four Hours, and putting them into an Earthen Glazed Vessel, pour good Vinegar on them, and cover it with a Board. Thus letting it stand for eight or ten Days: Then being taken out, and gently press'd, cast them into fresh Vinegar, and let them so remain as long as before. Repeat this a third time, and Barrel them up with Vinegar and a little Salt.[12]

Jalapeños en Escabeche

This Mediterranean-inspired dish was adapted in central and northern Mexico. It substitutes indigenous chillies for the fish used in the Old World.

Makes 3 one-pint (450-ml) jars

Vegetables

1 pound (450 g) jalapeños, in ¼- inch slices

4 large carrots, peeled and cut in ¼-inch slices

½ pound (225 g) small, white boiling onions, peeled

10 cloves garlic, peeled

1½ cup (20 ml) olive oil

Marinade

4 cups (950 ml) white vinegar

1 tbsp agave nectar

2 tbsp kosher salt

2 bay leaves

¼ tsp dried thyme leaves

¼ tsp dried oregano

In a large non-reactive pot, fry the vegetables separately in oil until the jalapeños have lost their dark green colour and are a bit caramelized, the carrots are firm but tender, the garlic has taken on a little colour and the onions are translucent. Set each vegetable aside as they are done. Return all cooked vegetables to the pot. Add marinade ingredients and bring to a boil. Lower the heat and simmer for ten minutes. Remove and discard bay leaves. Pack vegetables tightly into sterilized pint canning jars, fill with hot marinade, making sure that vegetables are covered with liquid. Process in a hot water bath for ten minutes. Allow to rest for at least a week before using.

Arabic mixture of lentils and rice (or other grain), while Spanish *Moros y Christianos* (Moors and Christians) is black beans and rice.

SIX

Beyond the Main Course

Foods That Must be Processed

One might think that people would have learned, long ago, to avoid eating things that are poisonous, or that the unwise would have been eliminated from the gene pool. It is not, however, so simple. Many cultures around the world have found ways to eat things that are bad for them, even deadly, without suffering ill effects.

Cooks in Western Europe know, for example, not to eat potatoes that have turned green (they contain glycoalkaloid toxins) or rhubarb leaves (they carry toxic levels of oxalic acid); that the seeds of several fruits (apples, cherries, apricots and peaches) contain cyanide; and even kidney beans – if eaten raw – have lectins that cause gastric distress. Insufficiently cooked fava beans cause favism – a form of anaemia that affects genetically susceptible people, primarily those from the Mediterranean region. We have all been told, since childhood, never to eat 'toadstools', or wild mushrooms, even though less than 5 per cent of them are dangerous. Cultural traditions preserve us from some of the less-pleasant properties of foodstuffs.

Other cultures have done the same with foods that are little known in the UK or U.S. Perhaps the most dramatic example is that of *fugu*, several species of Japanese blowfish in the *Takifugu* family. Parts of these fish contain lethal quantities of tetrodotoxin, which is far more powerful than potassium cyanide. There are no known antidotes, but poisoning victims are able to survive, on life support, until the tetrodotoxin is metabolized. *Fugu* must be prepared by specially trained and licensed chefs. Most *fugu* is consumed fresh, raw, but two forms qualify as preserved foods: dried fins used in a dish called *hire-zake*, and the fish's ovaries, which have extremely high levels of tetrodotoxin but are rendered safe for consumption by pickling in salt and rice bean paste, which contains plenty of lactic acid.

Iceland's *lerhákarl* and *skyrhákarl*, the preserved flesh of Greenland sharks and basking sharks, are particularly odorous. Their intense ammoniated scent comes from the decomposition of urea and poisonous levels of trimethylamine oxide (TMAO) that can only be removed by up to three months of fermentation, buried in sand, followed by another three of drying. Non-Scandinavians are probably wondering, 'Why bother?' – but Icelanders also have a taste for well-rotted skate.

We have already seen how Mesoamericans use nixtamalization to make corn more nutritious, but corn can be eaten without treatment; it is just not as nutritionally balanced. Other foods, however, must be treated before they can be eaten. Cassava, the starchy root of certain shrubs in the *Euphorbiaceae* family, is indigenous to South America. It was spread by sixteenth-century Portuguese traders, and is now a staple food in tropical regions around the globe. Before processing – into tapioca pearls or powder, the flaky fermented *gari* of West Africa, or the manioc meal of Brazil – it contains potentially fatal amounts of cyanide.

Taro's starchy tuber-like corm is another staple food in tropical regions. Indigenous to southern Asia, it is now widely grown in Africa and South America as well. It cannot be eaten raw, as it contains irritating calcium oxalate crystals. Their effect can be lessened by cooking or by soaking in cold water.

Sago starch can be obtained from the pith of certain palms (*Metroxylon* spp.) and cycads (*Cycas revoluta*), but the cycad-based

> ## Cassavie (1823)
>
> This root, before it come to be eaten, suffers a strange conversion; for, being an absolute poyson when 'tis gathered, by good ordering, comes to be wholsome and nourishing; and the manner of doing it is this: They wash the outside of the root clean, and lean it against a Wheel, whole sole is about a foot broad, and covered with Latine, made rough like a large Grater. The Wheel to be turned about with a foot, as a Cutler turnes his Wheel. And as it grates the root, it falls down in a large Trough, which is the receiver appointed for that purpose. This root thus grated, is as rank poyson, as can be made by the art of an Apothecary, of the most venomous simples he can put together: but being put into a strong piece of double Canvas, or Sackcloth, and prest hard, that all the juice be squeezed out, and then opened upon a cloath, and dried in the Sun, 'tis ready to make bread. And thus 'tis done.[1]

starch is poisonous until it has been ground and repeatedly washed. Their neurotoxins cause ALS, Parkinson's-like disorders, as well as several forms of cancer. Cycad seeds contain higher concentrations, and their cycasin toxins cannot be removed through washing, so they are never eaten. Once treated properly, however, sago starchfrom either source can be used as a thickener, or as tapioca-like pearls.

Cashews are related to poison ivy, and the shells of the nuts contain a group of urushiol-like toxins, anacardic acids. These must be carefully removed, and never burned, as even the smoke can cause severe dermatitis or lung irritation. Curiously, cashew fruit is non-toxic. The sweet cashew apple has been made into preserves and chutneys in India, and fermented into various alcoholic beverages in Goa, Mozambique, Sri Lanka, Tanzania and the Dutch West Indies.

Many foods *can* be eaten without processing, but are immeasurably improved through the process. John Evelyn addressed the issue at the end of the seventeenth century:

> We purposely, and *in transitu* only, take notice here of the Pickl'd, *Muriated*, or otherwise prepared Herbs; excepting some such Plants, and Proportions of them, as are of hard digestion, and not fit to be eaten altogether *Crude . . .* and among which I reckon *Ash-keys, Broom-buds* and *Pods, Haricos, Gurkems, Olives, Capers,* the Buds and Seeds of *Nasturtia, Young Wall-nuts, Pine-apples, Eringo, Cherries, Cornelians, Berberries, &c.* together with several Stalks, Roots, and Fruits; Ordinary Pot-herbs, *Anis, Cistus Hortorum, Horminum, Pulegium, Satureia, Thyme*; the intire Family of Pulse and *Legumena . . . Condites* and Preserves

French confiture pan, 19th century, used for making fruit preserves.

with *Sugar* by the Hand of Ladies . . . are easily prepare'd for an *Extemporary Collation*, or to Usher in, and Accompany other (more solid, tho' haply not more Agreeable) Dishes, as the Custom is.[2]

Almost all olives contain bitter oleuropein and phenolic compounds that make them unpalatable. These can be leached out by packing in salt, soaking in brine or a solution of lye, or simply several washes of plain water. European olives are also fermented by naturally occurring *lactobacilli*, which both preserve them and add a complex tanginess. California canned olives skip the fermentation step, so have a much milder flavour.

Foods That Wouldn't Even Exist Without Processing

Sugars are found in many forms in nature, but honey is the only one that exists in a pure state without the intervention of some sort of processing. It could be argued that even honey is processed, but by bees instead of humans. Most natural sugars quickly ferment or spoil without some form of preserving technology – even if it is merely removing their excess water through evaporation (which is essentially what honeybees do).

Cane sugar is probably the best-known sweetener – at least in the developed world. It became the leading form of sugar there primarily because of the use of slavery during the colonial period. The United States banned the international slave trade in 1808, although slavery itself was not completely abolished until 1865's Thirteenth Amendment was added to the Constitution. Cuba stopped importing African slaves in 1867. While trade in African slaves ended in British colonies in the 1830s, Brazil continued to use African and indigenous slaves – the so-called 'Red Gold'– to produce sugar until 1888. Newer technologies, and alternate sources of sucrose (for example, from sugar beets and sorghum) would in any case have eventually eliminated the need for slaves. Cane sugar is made by pressing the juice from the stalks, then evaporating it to eliminate the excess water. At various stages, several different sweeteners can be obtained. The familiar crystals drop out of solution and are then refined to pristine whiteness, leaving behind molasses. If the refining of sugar crystals is less thorough, the result is turbinado, or raw sugar. It tastes similar to brown sugar, which is merely white sugar to which varying amounts of molasses have been returned. As the molasses is further processed, extracting more sugar crystals, it becomes progressively darker and more bitter. The last stage is blackstrap molasses.

The British favourite, Lyle's Golden Syrup, was invented because of a shortage of supplies of raw sugar at the Lyle refinery in Plaistow, England, at the end of the nineteenth century. The company's chemist, Charles Eastick, was trying to find a way to extract more crystalline sucrose from waste treacle. He used hydrochloric acid, causing the sucrose to break into fructose and glucose. While he failed to get the sucrose he sought, he discovered a thick sweet syrup that would not crystallize. The reaction also created a small amount of salt, which gives Lyle's Golden Syrup a richer flavour than high-fructose corn syrup (which is also produced through acid hydrolysis). High-fructose corn syrup is a primary ingredient in thousands of processed foods. It is inexpensive (largely due to U.S. government subsidies to corn farmers), is sweeter than sucrose and its liquid form is convenient for mechanized mass-production lines. At one time, high-fructose corn syrup was part of Karo syrups, but public pressure over preceived health concerns resulted in its removal from all of their products (Karo Light, colourless, flavoured with vanilla; Karo Dark, deep brown, flavoured with molasses; Karo Pancake Syrup, a substitute for real maple syrup, containing caramel colour, salt, natural and artificial colours, plus the preservative potassium sorbate; and Karo Lite, similar to Karo Light, but with one-third fewer calories). The fructose in all of these syrups helps baked goods stay soft and moist, and gives ice cream a smoother texture. Corn and sugar cane are certainly not the only source of sweet syrups. Sorghum, sugar beets and even barley malt have all been pressed into service as syrups.

The idea of evaporating sap to increase the concentration of plant sugars, and prevent their spoilage due to yeasts or bacteria, has occurred all over the world. The ancient Romans boiled un-fermented grape must to make *carenum* (with one-third of the water removed), *defructum* (flavoured with figs or quinces, half of the water removed) and *sapa* (the densest, with two-thirds of the water eliminated). Apicius recommends *defructum* as a preservative for fruit.

The Greeks produced two versions of sapa: *siraeum* and *hepsema*. Italians still make sapa in Emilia-Romagna, Marche and Sardinia – where it is known as *saba*, and might be pressed from the fruits of a prickly pear cactus.

North American maple trees are tapped to collect their sweet sap, which is boiled to yield maple syrup, or further reduced to make maple cream and maple sugar. Originally, Europeans wanted maple sugar to resemble the neutral flavour of cane sugar, so the highest grades were those that were light in colour, with little of the distinctive maple taste. Today, we prize the flavour of the darker varieties, so the lower grades are often preferable to the fancier ones.

Further south, Mexicans make syrups from the juices of agave plants, although most of that sap is fermented to make tequila. Two separate species yield agave nectar, and they are processed with different methods. The thick cores of *Agave tequiliana* are harvested, trimmed of leaves and pressed. The juice is then cooked, converting fructosan to fructose, then further reduced to the desired viscosity and colouration, becoming darker and more deeply flavoured as it caramelizes. *Agave salmiana*, on the other hand, is neither cut down nor pressed. As soon as a hollow stalk appears over the core, it is cut off, allowing access to the sap (*aguamiel*, 'honey water') from the core. It is collected each day and

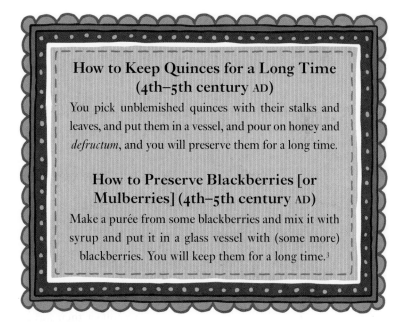

How to Keep Quinces for a Long Time (4th–5th century AD)

You pick unblemished quinces with their stalks and leaves, and put them in a vessel, and pour on honey and *defructum*, and you will preserve them for a long time.

How to Preserve Blackberries [or Mulberries] (4th–5th century AD)

Make a purée from some blackberries and mix it with syrup and put it in a glass vessel with (some more) blackberries. You will keep them for a long time.[3]

processed like *A. tequiliana*. A newer method substitutes unheated enzymatic fermentation, using *Aspergillus niger* mould.

In the Middle East, evaporation reduces fruit juices to several sweet molasses-like syrups. Arabic *dibs* and Turkish *pekmez* are syrups of grapes, figs or mulberries. Date syrup is *dibis. Dibs rumman* is better known, in the English-speaking world, as pomegranate molasses, although Turks call it *naşr ekisi*, and Azerbaijanis know it as *narşrab*. Pomegranate molasses is less sweet than cane molasses, but has a more interestingly tart flavour that comes from the fruit acids and tannins – the phenolic compounds that provide the 'dryness' of red wines and tea.

One of the most significant preserved forms of carbohydrates – culturally and economically – is neither syrup nor preserves (such as jams and jellies), but alcohol. Almost all of the world's fermented beverages come from two sources: natural sugars from fruits and some vegetables, or from plant starches converted to sugars by enzymes. Wines and their distilled versions, such as brandy, tequila and *eau de vie*, are examples of the former. Beers, whiskies and vodkas represent the latter. Western brewers use malts (produced by amylase already present in the grain), while in Asia they use red rice *koji* mould (*Aspergillus oryzae*). The same mould, called *qu* in Chinese, has been converting starches to fermentable sugars for over 2,000 years. *A. oryzae* is also used to make South Korean *soju*, a distilled liquor brewed from starch obtained from barley, potatoes, rice, sweet potatoes, *dangmil* (tapioca) or wheat.

Mouldy rice is not the most unusual source of amylase, however. We produce it in our own mouths. When we chew, our salivary glands squirt the enzyme ptyalin into our food. Ptyalin contains alpha-amylase, which – in the presence of calcium ions – converts some starches into sugars. You can experience this chemical reaction yourself; put some plain boiled rice in your mouth, and notice its initial flavour. After you chew it for a while, you will notice that it begins to taste sweeter.

In ancient times, one of the earliest methods for converting starches to fermentable sugars involved the chewing and subsequent expectoration of grains. Native peoples in Central and South America still use the technique to make *chicha*, a low-alcohol, partially fermented beer, from corn: 'The chicha maker chewed on maize to form small balls . . . The maize balls were left to dry and then made into a porridge, which was strained, boiled, and fermented for 3 to 6 days in large earthenware vats.'[4]

Modern breweries have replaced human mouths with *jora*, a malted form of corn that is sprouted in the dark so that it does not develop chlorophyll, then mashed. Unlike other malts, the corn is not dried or toasted. A Mexican beer, *tesguino*, uses *jora*.

Nepalese *tongba* beer is made with a special variety of millet (*Paspalum scrobiculatum*). African beers, brewed from millet or sorghum, are fermented twice: first by *lactobacilli*, followed by the typical yeast fermentation. Cooking stops the first fermentation before the mash becomes too sour, or uses up the sugars needed to make alcohol in the second fermentation. Several Sudanese beers (*merissas*) are made from sorghum and water, with varying preparations yielding very different brews.

Grain and fruits are not the only vegetative products that inventive brewers have converted to potable ethanol. Root beer, birch beer and sarsaparilla were originally fermented using the fragrant inner bark of various trees and, unlike the modern soft drinks of the same names, packed an alcoholic punch. Vodka can be made from potatoes but requires the addition of amylase, provided by a dose of barley malt (most commercial vodkas are made from grain, not potatoes).

Tofu (bean curd) is a uniform block of protein made from soya beans (the Burmese *to hpu* is similar, but made with chickpeas or yellow split peas). Pre-soaked dry beans are ground, then cooked in water to extract their 'milk'. The milk is strained, with the remaining solids set aside for other soya products, such as *tempeh* and *okara*. At this point, the process begins to resemble cheese-making. The strained protein- and oil-rich liquid is curdled with acidic salts (magnesium chloride with traces of magnesium sulphate), known in Japanese as *nigari*, and in Chinese as *lushui*. It is the residue left after seawater has evaporated, and the sodium chloride has been removed. Modern mass-producers use calcium sulphate, although some purists believe it affects the tofu's taste. Other acids, like vinegar (acetic) or citric (lemon juice) will coagulate the proteins in soya milk, creating varying degrees of firmness and flavour. Glucono delta-lactone (GDL), combined with water, becomes gluconic acid. Less sour than citric acid, it produces very soft, or silken, tofu. The enzyme papain can also curdle soya proteins for tofu, which seems counter-intuitive, since papain is best known as a meat tenderizer. The curds are then strained and pressed into blocks. Their degree of firmness is determined by how much water is pressed out. The tofu can be eaten as is, ice cold, with nothing but a splash of *shoyu* – Japanese soy sauce – and a few flakes of dried bonito, cooked in many ways or continue its transformation into other preserved foods.

Fresh tofu is similar to fresh dairy cheese, in that both are bland and perishable. Hence both are subjected to additional processes to make them last longer – and achieve a range of more complex flavours, aromas and textures. Tofu is often dried, either as an end in itself, or as a first step in producing different tofu products. Bean curd skin – the film that forms atop boiling soya milk like the skin on scalded cow's milk – is carefully removed, and dried into hard glossy sheets. When reconstituted in water, these become tender and slightly rubbery. Pressed seasoned bean curd – *dòu gān* – is briefly dried, then simmered in a mixture of soy sauce and five-spice powder. It is brown on the outside, creamy white on the inside, and firm enough to be sliced into thin noodle-like strips and eaten raw. Sometimes the tofu is dried under a blanket of hay, allowing airborne bacteria to ferment it. It is then reconstituted in a mixture of *yuan shai chi* (brown bean paste), chillies, salt water, *shao hsing* (Chinese wine) and vinegar. It is sometimes coloured with red yeast fungus (*Monascus purpureus*).

Preserved tofu, *fǔrǔ*, comes in several forms. Most are pickled in alcoholic brine of rice wine and salt, and may contain various spices. A strong version, called *tsui-fang*, is seasoned with chillies, cinnamon, dried shrimp, lemons and star anise – and sometimes sesame oil. *Hóngfǔrǔ* is similar, but coloured with red yeast fungus. *Chiang-doufu* is marinated in fermented soya bean paste or soy sauce for several days. Perhaps the most notorious form of preserved bean curd is *chòudòufu*, the aptly named 'stinky tofu'. It is pickled for months – in odoriferous bacterial brine – along with some combination of the following: amaranth greens, Chinese herbs, dried shrimp, meat, mustard greens and even spoiled milk. For the adventurous few who can get past the aroma, it's a delicacy.

As far a cry from stinky tofu as can be imagined is another food that must be processed before it can be consumed – but for which no one needs to struggle to form an 'acquired taste'. Chocolate begins as seeds inside large pods on small tropical trees. They are unpleasantly bitter, with none of the qualities we love about chocolate. The seeds are first fermented, then dried, roasted and cracked open to obtain the small brown nibs. Once the nibs have been ground into a paste, they are pressed into blocks. This was the form that the twelfth-century Mayans knew. It was consumed in the form of a spiced and frothy hot chocolate, made by whipping the bitter chocolate mass into hot water. By the fifteenth century, the Aztecs had adopted the drink, reserving it for their nobility. This concoction is what Hernando Cortés introduced to Europe after his Mexican Conquest. Bernal Díaz, a soldier in the service of Cortés, described the chocolate he saw in the court of Montezuma:

> From time to time they served him in cups of pure gold a certain drink made from cacao. It was said that it gave him power over women, but this I never saw. I did see them bring in more than fifty large pitchers of cacao with froth on it, and he drank some of it, the women serving with great reverence.[5]

By the end of the sixteenth century it had become popular in the Spanish court – in part because they added cinnamon and sugar, omitting the chillies preferred by Amerindians. Chocolate, as a hot beverage, remained a luxury item until the eighteenth century. By then, cacao plantations and cane sugar plantations, both manned by African slaves, had made both tropical ingredients less expensive.

In Holland, at about the same time, Casparus van Houten learned to separate cocoa butter from cocoa solids – the first step in the direction of creating chocolate bars. Early versions, made in Italy, were soon followed by more experiments in the Netherlands, Germany and Switzerland. Van Houten's son – Coenraad Johannes – learned how to modify cacao's natural bitterness with an alkali, and a British company (J. S. Fry & Sons, Ltd) figured out a way to recombine some of that dutched cocoa with

Ad for the original milk chocolate bars, produced over 50 years before the first Hershey Bar.

cocoa butter. For the first time, the world knew the joy of bars of sweet chocolate.

Conching – finely grinding heated chocolate – came next, from Rodolphe Lindt, a Swiss pharmacist turned chocolatier. Near the end of the nineteenth century, Henri Nestlé, a German-born Swiss pharmacist turned chemist turned food scientist, added dehydrated milk, inventing milk chocolate. A Mennonite from Pennsylvania, Milton Hershey, who had been manufacturing caramel candies, saw a demonstration of some German chocolate-making machines at Chicago's World's Fair (the 1893 Columbian Exposition celebrated the quadricentennial of the New World's discovery – the event that led to chocolate's worldwide popularity). Hershey immediately bought the equipment and set up shop in Lancaster County. Virtually all of the names of chocolate's early developers are still attached to their products.

Today, most of the world's cacao is grown in West Africa, often in conditions not much better than the old slave plantations of the sixteenth and seventeenth centuries, although in recent years the Fair Trade movement has been trying to reduce the use of child labour and other forms of forced labour. Chocolate is among the most cosmopolitan of preserved foods.

Condiments and Other Ingredients

The following foods are secondary only in the sense that they do not provide primary sustenance – they are not staple foods. Condiments and seasoning ingredients are responsible for the flavour profiles that define the world's cuisines. It is impossible to imagine Chinese cooking without fermented soybeans, or the cuisines of the Middle East without yoghurt.

Sweeteners constitute one of the primary categories of pantry staples. Plants produce virtually all sugars by converting sunlight, water and carbon dioxide into the carbohydrates that fuel most of the planet's life forms. We have already seen many of the better-known forms of sugar, but they are not alone, of course. For centuries people have also made sweet syrups from fruits as well. Swiss *raisinée* is made from apples, pears or whatever fruit is handy. Similar fruit syrups are known in France as *vin cuit*, and in Italy as *vincotto* – literally 'cooked wine'. Perhaps the largest category of sugar-based preserved food – although many don't even think of it *as* food – is candy. Some sweets are almost entirely sugar, with only traces of other ingredients: a bit of food colouring and an infinitesimal quantity of essential oil for flavouring. By controlling the temperature at which the sugar is processed; adding other ingredients, for example chocolate, fruits and nuts, plus less obvious substances such as milk powders, starches, gums, gelatine, preservatives, stabilizers, emulsifiers and even air; and monitoring how it is physically manipulated while it cools, an infinite number of variations are possible. Some have shelf-lifes of years, while others (such as those that feature chocolate) can only last if kept cool.

Vinegars, as we have seen, can be produced from anything that contains enough carbohydrate to ferment into alcohol. Traces of the original foods' tastes survive in the finished vinegar, so our kitchens may sport several varieties: wine vinegar (including varieties made from champagne and sherry); hard cider; beer and ale; or rice vinegars based on sake. Aside from the source of the original sugars, vinegars can be flavoured in a number of ways. Fruits, herbs and spices, left to macerate in relatively flavourless vinegars, can provide a wide spectrum of special vinegars. Raspberry vinegar, for example, was the darling of the culinary world back in the 1970s – for a long time afterwards, it was almost impossible *not* to be offered raspberry vinaigrette as an option on restaurant salads. Balsamic vinegar has had a somewhat longer presence in the market – despite the fact that many products sold as 'balsamic vinegar' in fact are not. True balsamic vinegar comes only from Modena and Reggio Emilia, and is made in a time-consuming manner: the must (pressed from the specific grape varietals Lambrusco, Sangiovese and Trebbiano) is cooked before fermenting to concentrate the sugars, some of which caramelize. After the must becomes wine vinegar, it is aged in a series of casks, each made of a different wood. Over a decade or more, the vinegar gradually thickens as water is lost through evaporation, and (like aged wine, whisky and brandy) it takes on wood flavours from the barrels. At each step, it becomes more complex, and loses some volume. That is why true balsamic vinegar is expensive. Cheap imitations are just vinegar, plus artificial flavours and caramel colouring – not even close to the real thing, a product that has been made the same way since the eleventh century.

Vinegar can even be produced in factories that have never seen any sort of vegetable product. So-called 'distilled vinegar' is harsh, and obviously lacks the character of the varieties described above. It is best reserved for cleaning, or acidulating water to prevent cut fruits and vegetables from browning – functions that do not affect the flavour of the finished dish.

Butter and olive oil are the two most-used fats – at least in the West. Butter is fairly delicate and prone to spoilage, as long as its water content is not significantly reduced, as with clarified butter. In India, butter is clarified to rid it of the water and milk solids that promote spoilage. This ghee keeps well, even without refrigeration, and has the advantage of not burning when used as a frying medium. Moroccans go a step further; they flavour clarified butter with salt and herbs (such as *za'atar*, various close relatives

Ghee: the original type, on the left, that is just clarified butter, and artificial ghee, on the right, made of hydrogenated vegetable oil (a margarine-like substance suitable for vegans).

of thyme and oregano) then pack it in stone jars to ripen. The result is fragrant fermented *smen*. It is aged from just one month to many years, becoming more intense as time passes. Perhaps it is not surprising that the French name for smen is *beurre rance*. It goes far beyond rancidity, to a complex funk reminiscent of aged cheese or Chinese stinky tofu. Moroccans are not alone in their love of fermented butter – it is known as *samneh* in Lebanon, and *niter kibbeh* in Ethiopia, where it is seasoned with a spicy mixture that might include black pepper, cardamom, garlic, ginger, fenugreek, onions and turmeric.

Salting helps sweet butter last a little longer, but refrigeration (or even freezing) is the only way to keep butter fresh for any significant length of time. It is important to wrap butter carefully, however, because it is very good at capturing scent molecules from the air. Improperly wrapped butter will absorb any odours present in one's refrigerator or freezer. Perfumers use this property of butter to fix the scents of flowers, which are later extracted by washing with alcohol.

Olive oils are graded by the degree to which the olives have been subjected to processing; the least processed – that is, the least amount of heat and chemicals needed to extract the oil – is the highest quality, cold-pressed extra virgin. In recent years, the high cost of extra virgin oil has led unscrupulous producers to mix oils from different places, only bottling them in Italy for marketing purposes. Some even crush leaves and twigs in the oil to add a green colour that suggests higher quality. Some cooks like to deep fry in extra virgin oil, despite the fact that the fruity or peppery qualities that distinguish such oils are destroyed by high heat. Cheaper light olive oils make more sense for such purposes. The very best oils should be reserved for salads and dipping or for finishing sauces. Infused oils – usually olive oil in which fragrant ingredients such as garlic, basil or truffles have been steeped – are usually added as a last-minute garnish. Dark-roasted sesame oil serves this purpose in Chinese cookery. Olive oil keeps better than

Smen (1790)

Common salt is almost the only substance that has been hitherto employed for the purpose of preserving butter; but I have found, by experience, that the following composition is, in many respects, preferable to it, as it not only preserves the butter more effectually from any taint of rancidity, but makes it also look better, and taste sweeter, richer and more marrowy, than if the same butter had been cured with common salt alone. . . . Take of sugar one part, of nitre one part, and of the best Spanish great salt . . . two parts. Beat the whole into a fine powder, mix them well together, and put them by for use.

Of this composition one ounce should be put to every sixteen ounces of butter; mix this salt thoroughly with the butter as soon as it has been freed from the milk, and put it without loss of time into the vessel prepared to receive it, pressing it so close as to leave no air-holes, or any kind of cavities within it. Smooth the surface, and if you expect that it will be above a day or two before you can add more, cover it close up with a piece of clean linen, and above that a piece of wetted parchment, or for want of them, fine linen that has been dipped in melted butter, that is exactly fitted to the vessel all round, so as to exclude the air as much as possible, without the assistance of any watery brine; when more butter is to be added, these coverings are to be taken off, and the butter applied close above the former, pressing it down and smoothing as before, and so on till the vessel be full. When it is quite full, let the two covers be spread over it with the greatest care, and let a little melted butter be poured around the edges, so as to fill up every cranny, and effectually exclude the air. A little salt may then be strewed over the whole, and the cover be firmly fixed down to remain close till it be opened for use. If all this be carefully done, the butter may be kept perfectly sound in this climate for many years. How many years I cannot tell, but I have seen it two years old, and in every respect as sweet and sound as when it was only a month old.[6]

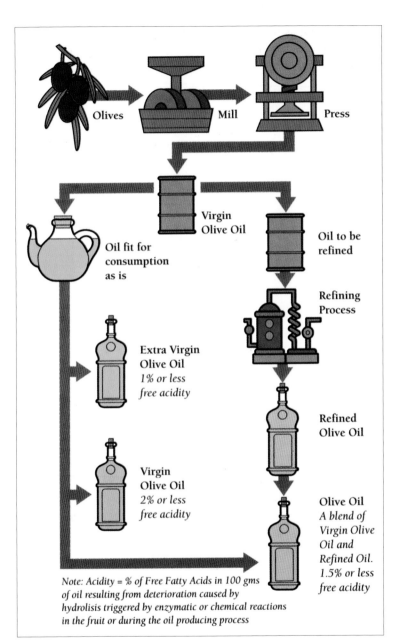

Olives

Mill

Press

Virgin Olive Oil

Oil fit for consumption as is

Oil to be refined

Refining Process

Extra Virgin Olive Oil
1% or less free acidity

Refined Olive Oil

Virgin Olive Oil
2% or less free acidity

Olive Oil
A blend of Virgin Olive Oil and Refined Oil. 1.5% or less free acidity

Note: Acidity = % of Free Fatty Acids in 100 gms of oil resulting from deterioration caused by hydrolisis triggered by enzymatic or chemical reactions in the fruit or during the oil producing process

Steps in the production of different grades of olive oil.

butter, so long as it remains protected from light and air. Even if sealed in an unopened tin, however, it will gradually develop the off-flavours of rancidity.

Like the best olive oils, certain oils are chosen specifically for their flavours – and tend to be added just before serving so those ephemeral flavours are not destroyed by cooking. Nut oils such as walnut, almond and hazelnut add subtle complexity to vinaigrettes. Most nut oils need to be refrigerated, or used soon after pressing, because they become rancid faster than other vegetable oils. Soya oil has the highest smoke point among the most-used cooking oils at 238°C (460°F), so it is the preferred frying medium in Chinese restaurants. It is also relatively inexpensive. Home cooks usually prefer peanut oil, however, as even though its smoke point is not quite as high, at 225°C (437°F), it tastes better.

Coconut oil, however, is actually aged as part of its production. Crushed coconut meat is fermented in water, which breaks down the walls of the fat cells, freeing the oil to rise to the surface for collection. Alternatively, this wet method can employ enzymes, recreating, chemically, what is accomplished by fermentation. Coconut oil can also be produced by pressing sun-dried coconut meat, copra, or by extracting the oil with solvents, such as hexane. The oil is rich in saturated fats; it stores well, solidifies at room temperature and produces very crisp fried foods.

Rendered chicken or goose fat, flavoured with onions, is *schmaltz* – a standard ingredient and condiment among Eastern Europe's Ashkenazy Jews. Religious dietary laws prohibit the simultaneous use of meat and dairy, so *schmaltz* takes the place of butter on tables where meat is served. *Schmaltz* replaced the olive or sesame oils that would normally be used by the Sephardim to the south. Rendering *schmaltz* also produces a garnish of crisp and tasty bits of onion, skin and connective tissue. *Gribenes* are the Jewish equivalent of American Southerners' 'cracklins'.

Little jars of all kinds of preserved pastes are used, every day, almost everywhere. They include nut pastes: the familiar peanut butter, and Nutella; soy, almond, cashew, pistachio and sunflower seed butters; but also tahini and Chinese sesame paste. Cooks employ flavour-enhancing pastes made from prawns or anchovies, olives (tapenade), or even spent yeast (Marmite).

Dishes can be spiced with Thai curry pastes, Moroccan *harissa*, Indonesian *sambal oelek*, or Mexican *chipotle en adobo*. Chinese chilli paste with garlic, and a wide range of bean pastes, such as Chinese *chiang* and Korean *gochujang*, practically define Asian cooking. Soy sauce is the prototypical preserved food. Familiar to Westerners as a condiment on the table in Chinese and Japanese restaurants, it serves a much greater role in many of the world's kitchens. Salt accentuates other flavours, and soy sauce is often the only source of salt in Asian dishes. In basic terms, it is soybeans (and sometimes wheat), fermented in brine and helped along by certain moulds. Its proteins become hydrolysed, creating various glutamates. Glutamates are compounds that 'accent' inherent tastes and add savoury umami. The proteins in industrial soy sauce are merely hydrolysed by acids, then salt and caramel colouring are added, forming a liquid that bears only a slight resemblance to true soy sauce.

Canned coconut milk, popular throughout South and Southeast Asia, as well as in Brazil and the Caribbean.

Different kinds of genuine soy sauce derive their qualities from slight variations in the time and temperature of the brewing, filtering, salt ratios in the brine and additional ingredients. Soy sauce is the result of a cascade of complex fermentations that begin when *Aspergillus* moulds (*A. oryzae* and *A. sojae*) break down proteins into more basic components of amino acids and sugars. *Saccharomyces cerevisiae* – the same yeast used in brewing wines and beers – converts some of the sugars into alcohol, which then reacts with some of the amino acids to form still more flavouring compounds. After brine is added, *Lactobacillus* breaks down some of the remaining sugars as well, adding the tartness of lactic acid. The multiplicity of generated compounds makes real soy sauce taste better than the one-dimensional industrial versions. Once the desired level of fermentation has occurred, the sauce is pressed to remove solids, and filtered and pasteurized to kill any yeasts, moulds and bacteria remaining in the liquid. The soy sauce is either bottled for immediate use, or set aside for ageing.

Soy sauce was, at first, a by-product in the manufacture of fermented bean pastes, called *mien chiang*, in China. Chinese naturally brewed soy, with no additives, still predominates the world market, although Japanese and artificial types are more common in the U.S. Chinese soy sauces are produced in a continuum of flavours and colours, starting with light or thin soy, *jiàngyóu* (not to be confused with 'Lite Soy', a low-sodium version often seen in the West). Light soy is paler in colour and higher in salt than other soy sauces; it is the primary version used in cooking.

Light soy appears in a few variations as well. *Xiā zǐ jiàngyóu* is flavoured with shrimp, *baijiu* (a distilled liquor made from sorghum) and sugar. If light soy is used in place of brine to make soy sauce, the richer result is called *shuānghuáng*. Singaporean light soy is called *jiàngqīng*; Vietnamese is *xì dầu*. In Taiwan, a slightly darker sauce made without grain, and with just salt instead of brine, *yìnyóu*, is fermented longer than the other Chinese soys already mentioned. A more deeply flavoured and coloured Chinese soy – *lǎochōu*, dark or black soy – is thicker than the soys we have discussed, and it has a strong molasses component. The thick soy *jiàngyóugāo* is much the same but additional sugar and starch give it more body than dark soy (the Burmese equivalent is called *kya nyo*). Mushroom soy, *cǎogū lǎochōu*, is dark soy that has

Green curry paste. One of the four primary seasoning pastes used in Thai cooking, this one contains chillies, coriander (cilantro), garlic, lemongrass, lime leaves, onion and other spices, plus some fermented products: fish sauce and shrimp paste.

been cooked along with straw mushrooms (which Walt Disney's dancing mushrooms in *Fantasia* resemble).

Like Chinese soy, Japanese *shoyu* comes in a spectrum of flavours and colours progressing from light to dark. Shoyu uses more wheat than does Chinese soy. Sweet *shiro* (Japanese for 'white'), for example, uses practically no soya beans. *Usukuchi* is like Chinese thin soy; it is light-coloured and quite salty. *Saishikomi* is similar to Chinese *shuānghuáng*, in that it uses *usukuchi* in place of brine in the brewing.

The most distinctive *shoyu* is *tamari*; it is made with all (or almost all) soya beans, and has the deepest colour and flavour of the Japanese soy sauces. *Tamari* is created in the process of making miso, and its distinctive flavour results from fermenting with a different species of mould: *Aspergillus tamari tamarii*. *Joseon ganjang*, a similar by-product of fermented bean paste, *doenjang*, is one of the defining ingredients in Korean cooking.

Like German wines, Indonesian soy sauces are categorized according to their sugar content. The 'driest' is the salty *kecap asin*, corresponding to Chinese thin soy (although all Indonesian soys are thicker and more strongly flavoured than those from China). *Kecap manis sedang* is sweeter, but not as thick as *kecap asin*. At the far end of the soy spectrum, *kecap manis*, containing palm sugar, is the sweetest and thickest Indonesian soy. It is also the least salty of the three types. Soy sauces are important in other regions, sometimes in similar forms, sometimes with curious variations. Asian migrations have influenced the cooking of several places, some more obvious than others. The Philippines and Hawaii, of course (athough in the Philippines, a national taste for sour flavours leads to a combination of their soy, *toyo*, with the juice of very sour citrus fruits), but many Japanese settled in Brazil as well.

Sambal nasi goreng – a Dutch-Indonesian seasoning paste made of onions, vegetable oil, salt, ground chillies, garlic, shrimp paste and dark soy. It's the Dutch equivalent of English 'curry powder' – not in flavour, but in that both are simplified culinary reminders of a colonial past.

Brazilian soy sauce is similar to *shoyu*, but – as wheat does not grow well near the equator – it is made with corn and soybeans.

Perhaps the most unusual take on 'soy sauce' is Singapore's *angmo daoiu*, which is Southern Min for 'white' – literally 'red-haired' – 'man's soy sauce' (*angmo* is a racial epithet denigrating Caucasians). *Angmo daoiu* is, in fact, a name for Worcestershire sauce! A more ethnically neutral term – *la jiangyou* ('spicy soy sauce') – is preferred in Shanghai.

Roman legions occupied a town in England that was later an Anglo-Saxon village, Weorgoran ceaster (settlement of the people by the winding river). That town later became known as Worcester. 'Worcestershire' means 'the county where the Weorgorans' village was'. The name 'Worcestershire sauce' acknowledges the

Lea & Perrins' Sauce trade card, late 19th century.

location of the Lea & Perrins factory in 1838. Regional names for Worcestershire sauce reflect its British origins: in Brazil, *molho ingles*; in Indonesia, *kecap inggris*; and in Honduras, *salsa inglesa*.

In one account of the sauce's history, when a failed liquid spice mixture was unpleasantly strong, its barrel was put aside and forgotten. A year or so later, it was tasted and found to have become the deeply flavoured sauce we know today. Fermentation had done the trick. The story is probably apocryphal, since many other fermented products boast similar serendipitous origins. Curiously, Worcestershire sauce is an English modification of Southeast Asian fish sauces, and, in the process, revived a Western sauce that mirrors Roman *garum* and *liquamen*. So the modern sauce might actually have seemed familiar to the Roman soldiers stationed in England centuries ago. Gentlemen's Relish (or *patum peperium*) is a thicker, anchovy-rich fermented condiment made by Britain's Elsenham Quality Foods. A Niçoise variant, *pissalat* – a paste of anchovies in olive oil – is flavoured with bay leaves, black pepper, cloves and thyme. One can almost follow the spoor of ancient Roman armies by the lingering aroma of decomposing anchovies.

Worcestershire sauce had another predecessor – somewhat more recent than the Roman Empire. A century before Messrs Lea & Perrins entered the sauce-making trade, a man named Peter Harvey stumbled upon a similar condiment. While the exact recipe of his eponymous sauce was proprietary, several reverse-engineered recipes were in circulation.

Harvey's Sauce was marketed by a brother-in-law named Lazenby, who was less than thrilled by the numerous imitations of their family's intellectual property. The company ran this warning advert in the 6 April 1855 issue of the *Glasgow Herald*: 'none is genuine but that which bears the name WILLIAM LAZENBY on the back of each bottle, in addition to the front label used so many years, and signed ELIZABETH LAZENBY.'

Harvey's Sauce (1840)

Dissolve six anchovies in a pint of strong vinegar, and then add to them three table-spoonfuls of India soy, and three table-spoonfuls of mushroom catchup, two heads of garlic bruised small, and a quarter of an ounce of cayenne. Add sufficient cochineal powder to colour the mixture red. Let all these ingredients infuse in the vinegar for a fortnight, shaking it every day, and then strain and bottle it for use. Let the bottles be small, and cover the corks with leather.[7]

Fermented fish sauces are part of a spectrum of products used in many cultures: *budu*, a Malaysian one made from anchovies; *nam pla*, a generic name in use from the Philippines to Cambodia; *padaek*, made from freshwater fish in landlocked Laos; *pla ra*, a Thai sauce made from snakehead murrel (*Channa striata*); and *hao you*, the familiar Chinese oyster sauce.

Moving from the possibly putrid to the profoundly piquant, thousands of hot pepper sauces are marketed, and avidly consumed, today. They range from barely spicy to mind- and mouth-shatteringly hot. Tabasco (perhaps the most famous example) is not even close to being the hottest, but is still among the most popular. It is produced today just as it was shortly after the American Civil War ended:

> fresh peppers are mashed, mixed with a small amount of Avery Island salt extracted from the salt mines that lie beneath the Island, and placed in oak barrels. The wooden barrel tops are covered with more Avery Island salt to form a natural protective barrier, and the pepper mash is allowed to age for up to three years.[8]

The sauce is later combined with vinegar, strained and poured into their signature small bottles – patterned after the used cologne bottles that Edmund McIlhenny, Tabasco's founder, refilled as his first commercial samples in 1868.

Tabasco may be a quintessentially American sauce, but the one most associated with U.S. foods is ketchup – which, ironically, is not an American invention at all. The thick, red, tomato/spice/vinegar condiment does not even resemble its ancestors. In the eighteenth century, British cooks attempted to recreate *kecap* or *ketjap*, the thick, sweet soy sauce brought back from Malaysia, by adapting it with English ingredients such as mushrooms and walnuts. Before that, the Malaysians had adapted theirs from a Chinese fermented sauce. A century earlier,

Advertisement
for Heinz Tomato
Ketchup, c. 1934.

Chinese *kê-chiap* was brewed from fish and salt. What none of these sauciers realized was that they were recreating similar rich umami flavours by developing glutamates – naturally present in very different ingredients – through fermentation.

By the beginning of the nineteenth century, tomatoes began to appear in recipes for 'catsup'. Mary Randolph – a neighbour and relative by marriage of Thomas Jefferson – published

To Make Catchup (1747)

Take the large flaps of mushrooms, pick nothing but the straws and dirt from it, then lay them in a broad earthen pan, strew a good deal of salt over them, let them lie till next morning, then with your hand break them, put them into a stewpan, let them boil a minute or two, then strain them though a coarse cloth, and wring it hard. Take out all the juice, let it settle, then pour it off clear, run it through a thick flannel bag, (some filter it through brown paper, but that is a very tedious way) then boil it; to a quart of the liquor put a quarter of an ounce of whole ginger, and half a quarter of an ounce of whole pepper. Boil it briskly a quarter of an hour, then strain it, and when it is cold, put it into pint bottles. In each bottle put four or five blades of mace, and six cloves, cork it tight; and it will keep two years. This gives the best flavour of the mushrooms to any sauce. If you put to a pint of this catchup a pint of mum [a German malt liquor that was popular in Glasse's time], it will taste like foreign catchup.[9]

recipes for catsup based on mushrooms and oysters, but also one with tomatoes, given here. Randolph had no way of knowing that tomatoes are also good sources of the glutamates that made the other catsups so savoury. Shortly thereafter, catsups became sweeter, with added sugar and spices – like cinnamon and clove. Most of today's catsups have preserved that flavour

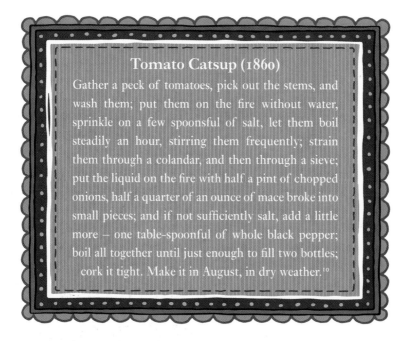

Tomato Catsup (1860)

Gather a peck of tomatoes, pick out the stems, and wash them; put them on the fire without water, sprinkle on a few spoonsful of salt, let them boil steadily an hour, stirring them frequently; strain them through a colandar, and then through a sieve; put the liquid on the fire with half a pint of chopped onions, half a quarter of an ounce of mace broke into small pieces; and if not sufficiently salt, add a little more – one table-spoonful of whole black pepper; boil all together until just enough to fill two bottles; cork it tight. Make it in August, in dry weather.[10]

profile, along with a little vinegar – but substitute corn syrup for the sugar.

Surely, ketchup's co-regent in the kingdom of condiments is mustard. Prepared mustard has been sitting on our tables for a very long time. Apicius in the fourth century CE wrote of a number of condiments for meats, including mustard, but they are thinner – more like vinaigrette – than what we would think of as mustard today.

Curiously enough, mustard seeds themselves do not become hot until they are prepared, either from whole seeds or milled mustard flour, or even Tewkesbury mustard balls (dried lumps of powdered mustard and grated horseradish, a portable form used before Shakespeare's time, meant for reconstitution). *Sinâb* is a condiment that would not look out of place on a modern table – not as old as Apicius, perhaps, but written long before Falstaff mentioned it in *Henry IV, Part II*.

Mustard (13th century)

It is fitting to avoid old mustard seed, because if it is old, it acquires a bitterness, and for this reason it should be washed first with hot water and then made. Fresh mustard need not be washed, because it adds sharpness without bitterness.

How It Is Made: Take fresh mustard seeds and pound them a little in a mortar of stone or wood until they are crushed. Wash it with hot water so the bitterness departs, and drain out this water. Then return it to the mortar and crush it hard, sprinkling with sharp vinegar little by little. Then squeeze it in a piece of thick cloth or a rough wool apron. Then continue to pound it until it is disintegrated, and squeeze it until it comes out like fine talbîna [dissolved starch].

Then pound sweet, peeled almonds very hard, until they become like dough, and macerate until dissolved so that it moderates its bitterness, make it [the mustard] white and let it gain dregs and sweetness, because of the coolness and sweetness of the almonds. This is the benefit of the almonds, and their use to the mustard.

When this recipe is complete, use it in kebabs and other heavy, fatty foods, God willing.[1]

Further south, other hot condiments, such as North African harissa and *berbere*, did not require the services of mustard, at least once the New World's chillies became available. Harissa contains caraway seed, coriander (cilantro), coriander seed, garlic and mint, while Ethiopian *berbere* includes some combination of allspice, basil, bishop's weed, black pepper, cardamom, cinnamon, cloves, coriander, cumin, fenugreek, garlic, ginger, onions, nutmeg, rue and turmeric. Both are preserved with olive oil and salt.

Latin American salsas accompany meats, enliven starches and serve as dips for crisply fried snack foods. They provoke the appetite in a way that parallels the thin Indian chutneys served at the beginning of a meal – but they replace Old World ingredients like tamarind and yoghurt with the New World standards of tomatoes and chillies. Both are likely to include garlic, onions and sometimes coriander. Salsas, in their native countries, are made fresh,

Sinâb (13th century)

Clean good mustard and wash it with water several times. Then dry them and pound them until they are as fine as kohl [ash]. Sift it with a sieve of hair, and then pound shelled almonds and put them with the mustard and stir them together. Then press out their oil and knead them with breadcrumbs little by little, not putting in the breadcrumbs all at once but only little by little.

Then pour strong vinegar, white of color, over this dough for the dish, having dissolved sufficient salt in the vinegar. Then mix it well to the desired point, and strain it thoroughly with a clean cloth. And there are those who after it is strained add a little honey to lessen its heat. Either way it is good.[12]

Mild Tomato Chipotle Salsa

For a spicier salsa, just increase the amount of chipotles in the recipe.

Makes 6 pints

9 cups (2.25 kg) tomatoes, peeled, chopped and seeded
6 cups (750 g) green peppers, chopped and seeded
1 can (215 g/7.5 oz) chipotles in adobo, puréed
3 cloves garlic, roasted and crushed to a paste
1 tbsp *piloncillo*, or brown sugar
1 cup (250ml) red wine vinegar
salt to taste

Place the tomatoes and green peppers in a sieve over a bowl, allowing excess liquid to drain. In a large non-reactive saucepan, combine chipotle, garlic, sugar and vinegar. Add the tomatoes and peppers to the pot and mix well. Stirring frequently, bring to a full rolling boil. Adjust seasoning, adding salt as needed (keep in mind that the salsa will probably be served with salted tortilla chips). Pack into hot sterilized jars, leaving 1 cm (½ inch) of headspace. Process in a hot water bath for ten minutes.

but are more likely to be found in American markets ready made and packaged in squat jars (presumably to discourage tipping by inebriated tortilla chip consumers). A few years ago, salsas made culinary history by out-selling ketchup in the U.S. Impressive, certainly, but it must be noted that the statistic was based on price, not volume of each condiment.

Pickling – whether fermenting with salt and *lactobacilli*, or simply marinating in an acidic solution – has been a tried-and-true vegetable preserving method for millennia. Five thousand years ago, Mesopotamians and Egyptians made pickles (similar Arabic pickles, *mekhallel*, are still made from assorted vegetables, olives and lemons). They can be sweet and spicy, like bread and butter pickles, or pickled watermelon rind. They can be hot with a vinegar bite – like Italian *peperoncini*, or *giardiniera* (whole tabasco peppers) – or just barely hot, like cherry peppers. They can be as hot and salty as Indian pickles. They can be homemade, or produced in huge factories that stuff them into jars with sodium benzoate and/or EDTA to discourage any unapproved biological hanky-panky.

The first European to see what is now New York was an explorer who had been a pickle-maker: Amerigo Vespucci. Nevertheless, pickles were not made in the New World until the

Colman's powdered mustard, which only develops its heat when mixed with water.

This Indiana factory produced pickles and vinegar in the first third of the 20th century.

seventeenth century. The Dutch brought pickle recipes to New Amsterdam, and had large cucumber farms in what is now Brooklyn. New Yorkers had to wait nearly 200 years to enjoy the iconic sour or half-sours of the Lower East Side. They came along with the massive immigration of Central European Jews, who added a key ingredient to the pickle barrels: garlic.

For many people, 'pickles' are synonymous with 'cucumbers', and not just the big fermented ones. There are all kinds of cucumbers pickled in vinegar, dill being the most common. They may be whole, sliced into spears or cut cross-wise into discs. They may be spicy, sour, sweet or any combination of the above. They can be very mild, like the Chinese ribbons of cucumber softened by salt, and seasoned with sugar, ginger and tiny amount of fresh chillies. They may be huge, full-grown cukes, tiny – like sour French *cornichons* that relieve the unctuous fat of pâté – or sweet, as American gherkins are. They may even be chopped into tiny bits to make relish.

Piccalilli and chow-chow are examples of chopped pickle relishes, but with substantial regional variation. The British piccalillis are Anglicized versions of some Indian pickles, which are, as you might imagine, considerably less spicy and intense than their inspiration. The primary connection to the subcontinent is the presence of turmeric, which provides the mixture's yellow colour. All the other ingredients are distinctly European: cauliflower, summer squashes and lots of prepared mustard. Across the Atlantic, the British vegetables are replaced by sweet red and green peppers, and – near Chicago – chopped bright green pickled cucumbers. As one heads south, the piccalilli gives way to chow-chow, which adds chopped cabbage, onions, green tomatoes and other vegetables to the peppers of piccalilli.

Achars are the pickles British cooks tried to emulate with piccalilli. They derive their longevity not only from salt, but from the addition of oil and various acids, from citrus juice or tamarind pulp. They begin with sour fruits, such as citrus or underripe mangoes. *Achars* are intensely flavoured and pungent, igniting salty and sour explosions with each bite of fermented lemon, lime, mango or pea aubergine. Mrs Ali, writing in the days of the Raj, described the beginning of the pickle-making process: 'The young mangoes are gathered for preserves and pickles before the stone is formed; the full-grown unripe fruit is peeled, split, and dried, for seasoning curries, &c.'[13]

Achars represent the historical influence of Chinese, Indian, Malaysian and Spanish cultures on the Philippine islands. Shredded papayas and vegetables (peppers and carrots) are partly

Chow-chow

Chow-chow was almost always on my grandmother's table in Texas – although this version is based on a recipe in Kendra Bailey Morris's book *White Trash Gatherings: From-scratch Cooking for Down-home Entertaining*

Makes approx. 3.75 litres (8 pints)

For the vegetables
4 cups (500 g) white cabbage, cored
4 cups (250 g) mixed red and green bell peppers
2 cups (300 g) Vidalia (or other sweet) onions
3 jalapeño chillies
5 cucumbers, peeled and seeded
4 cups (1 kg) green tomatoes, cored
3 tbsp sea (kosher) salt

For the pickle
2 cups (500 ml) vinegar
1 cup (200 g) sugar
4 tbsp mustard seed
2 tbsp celery seed

Dice the vegetables, place them in a large non-reactive bowl, add salt, mix thoroughly, then place in the refrigerator for eight to twelve hours, tightly covered with plastic wrap. Rinse the vegetables and allow them to drain. Combine the pickling ingredients in a large pot, and boil until the sugar is completely dissolved. Add the vegetables and cook for about ten minutes. Pack into sterilized canning jars, seal and process in a water-bath for ten minutes.

dried, then cooked with vinegar, pineapple juice, raisins spices (mostly ginger) and sugar. After resting for a day or so, the *acharas* age in the refrigerator. Indonesian, Malaysian and Singaporean *acars* substitute cabbage, carrots and yard-long beans. They are pickled in vinegar and chillies, then thickened with ground peanuts. Southeast Asian variations on the *achar* theme feature vegetables that are virtually unknown outside of the region: *gunda* (*Cordia* spp.); *kerda* (*Capparis decidua*); *karela* (bitter gourd/melon) (*Momordica charantia*); *karonda* (*Carissa carandas*); jackfruit (*Artocarpus heterophyllus*); lotus stem (*Trapa* spp.); and *zimikand* (purple yam, *Dioscorea alata*).

Brinjal relish: salted and heavily spiced Indian aubergine (eggplant) pickle.

The Dutch side dish *atjar tjampoer* uses shredded vegetables also, but these are typically Dutch vegetables (cabbage, carrots and cauliflower), seasoned with peppery Indonesian *sambal oelek*, plus ginger, sugar, turmeric and vinegar. According to the Dutch culinary historian Karin Vaneker, 'In general, colonizers weren't interested in developing local agriculture . . . [they] likely tried to cultivate European crops.'[14] Wars and colonial exploitation are collisions of cultures. One of the few positive outcomes of these unfortunate events is the creation of new foodstuffs. When life gives you lemons, make lemon pickle.

The Japanese make and consume many types of pickles, often as traditional accompaniments to rice or sushi and sashimi. *Gari* is the familiar sliced ginger with a sweet tanginess that sits next to the wasabi on a sushi platter. It is often dyed pale pink to recall the colour of very young ginger. Many Japanese pickles begin their production with other fermented ingredients. *Beni shoga* is tender young ginger pickled in vinegar formerly used for pickling *umeboshi* – incredibly salty, sour dried plums. *Narazuke* are deeply coloured and flavoured vegetables that have been aged in the sediment from making sake. *Fukujinzuke* – a chopped mixed pickle of cucumber, daikon radish, eggplant and lotus root – is marinated in a mixture of *shoyu* and *mirin* (sweetened rice wine).

Chutneys are the sweet cousins of Indian pickles. Unlike Indian pickles, chutneys feature ripe fruits. The famous 'Major Grey's' uses sweet ripe mangoes.

For sweetness, it is hard to beat confits, jams, jellies and preserves. Greeks even serve thick sugary fruit as a spoonable dessert all by itself. They call it *glyko* (from the same root as our words for other sweet substances: glucose and glycogen). *Glyko* can be made from apples, apricots, cherries, figs, lemons, orange peel, quinces, strawberries, watermelon rind and even green walnuts – virtually any available fruit.

Lemon *achar*, a mason jar of heavily spiced Indian pickle, fermenting in mustard oil on a sunny windowsill.

Outside of Greece and its neighbours, we are more likely to think of these sweet pectin-thickened fruit products as something to spread on toast, a muffin or a croissant – or pair with peanut butter.

Marmalades are very old. Apicius includes recipes for quinces preserved in a mixture of honey and difructum, and the name itself may be derived from the Greek *melimelon*, which means 'honeyed fruit'. Portuguese *marmelada*, for a sweet quince preserve made at least as early as the fifteenth century, also has a valid claim on marmalade's etymology.

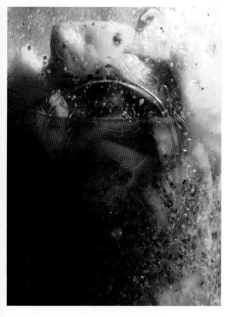

Our herb and spice shelves are filled with dried, and sometimes fermented, foodstuffs. There is no clear distinction between herbs and spices, but generally herbs utilize the foliage and flowers of plants, while spices are produced from the bark, fruit, seeds and roots. Some herbs and spices become stronger when dried, because their essential oils and other aromatic compounds are concentrated, while others lose strength

Green Tomato Chutney

This recipe, adapted from one in the 1975 edition of *The Joy of Cooking*, is deep-brown, thick, fragrant and luscious. It is warm with spices, yet not hot. It is tangy from the unripe tomatoes, lime and vinegar, but not exactly sour – as the fruit, molasses and sugar cut the acidic bite. High acidity and sugar content make this a pretty safe item for beginners.

Makes 3 pints (1.4 litres)

2 lb (900 g) green tomatoes, coarsely chopped

2 garlic cloves, chopped

1 lime, chopped

2 cups (200 g) raisins

1.5 lb (700 g) sugar

⅓ cup (80 ml) molasses

2.5 oz (70 g) fresh ginger, peeled and chopped

1 tsp Laos (powdered galangal)

½ tbsp sea (kosher) salt (not iodized)

12 fl. oz (350 ml) cider vinegar

1 oz (28 g) brown mustard seed

2 fresh jalapeño chillies, seeded and chopped

Combine all ingredients in a non-reactive pot, large enough to permit stirring. Bring to a boil, then turn down to a simmer for about two hours. Stir frequently to prevent burning at the bottom. It is done when the mixture has thickened and reduced to 1.7 litres (6 cups). Pack into hot, sterilized jars and seal, then process for fifteen minutes in boiling water to cover. Cool, check to see that the seals are sound, and store in a cool, dry place. If the seals aren't perfect, reprocess or store in the refrigerator.

Note: The chutney will continue to thicken as it cools, so don't judge its viscosity while it is hot. If you find the chutney too thick when you open a jar, you can always adjust the consistency with a little water.

Nectarine Chutney

This chutney was adapted from the recipe for American Peach Chutney in the 4th edition of *Putting Food By*. It is spicier and tastes a bit more Indian than American.

For the pickle:
1 quart (1 litre) apple cider vinegar
2 lemons, seeded and coarsely chopped, including juice
2 lb (1 kg) jaggery (or substitute dark brown sugar)
2 garlic cloves, coarsely chopped
1½ tbsp nigella seeds
½ oz (15 g) brown mustard seeds
½ tsp cayenne pepper
½ tsp cinnamon
1½ tbsp sea (kosher) salt
1 cup (275 g) crystallized ginger, coarsely chopped
3 serrano chilli peppers, seeded and chopped

Fruit:
4 lb (2 kg) nectarines, seeded and chopped into chunks
8 dried Medjool dates, pitted and chopped
1 tbsp mustard oil

Combine all pickle ingredients in a heavy non-reactive pot. Boil the mixture over medium heat for 30 minutes, stirring occasionally. Add the fruit ingredients and cook over a medium heat, stirring occasionally, until the chutney is tender and somewhat thickened (45–60 minutes). Pack into hot, sterilized pint jars, and process in a boiling water bath for ten minutes.

Note: You can find nigella seeds and mustard oil in Indian groceries (and some health food stores).

Advertisement for pectin used in making home-made jam, 1940s. Because of the Second World War, sugar was still in short supply.

through the evaporation of volatile substances. The drying process often significantly alters flavour profiles of these plant parts as well. Dried root ginger is hotter and less aromatic than its fresh version. Tarragon loses some of its anise aroma when dried, but adds the hay-like scent of coumarin, produced by fermentation during the drying process.

Peppercorns (*Piper nigrum*) come in three basic forms: white, black and green. White peppercorns have had their skin removed before drying. It has most of the heat of pepper, but not much of the aromatic quality of black and green peppers. Their characters are due to compounds present in the berries' skins. Green peppercorns have a slightly resinous quality that can be preserved either by freeze-drying or by pickling in brine. Black pepper has the most complex flavour and aroma because the peppercorns are fermented in their skins before drying, allowing the formation of dozens of subtle flavouring compounds.

Only immature vanilla beans – the fruit of a tropical orchid – are used, as ripe ones split to drop the seeds and have no

Making marmalade. As it cooks, the peel becomes transluscent. The peel contains pectin that forms the thickening gel, so – unlike preserves made from many other fruits – no pectin need be added.

Preserved Strawberries (1727)

To one pound of ripe strawberries put one pound of powdered loaf sugar, laying alternately on a deep dish a layer of each. Let them remain thus for twenty-four hours, when boil them in a sirup till they are all of a color. In order to determine when they are done enough, cut one of them open. Then, taking them out, boil the sirup to the consistence of a jelly, let it remain till cool, then put in your strawberries, and let them boil up once, take them off, and when cool, put them into a pot for use.[15]

---

value. Their flavour develops through fermentation by special heat-tolerant bacteria. Vanilla is commonly used in the form of a tincture in alcohol, known as an extract. Natural vanilla contains some 130 compounds, which provide the extract's complex, beguiling flavour, while artificial extract has just synthetic vanillin and alcohol. Most salted and/or fermented fruit and vegetable products are intended for use as ingredients in cooking, rather than for eating directly. The Greeks have been preserving lemons since the first century CE. Brine-cured lemons are important ingredients, or condiments, in North Africa, India and parts of Southeast Asia.

Chinese salted black soya beans, *douchi*, are not the same as the black (or turtle) beans known in the West. Well-known for over 2,000 years, these fermented soybeans have a sweet–salty and slightly bitter flavour, and an intriguing aroma that pairs beautifully with green ginger in black bean sauce, either fresh or ready-made in a jar. The beans sometimes include fragrant bits of dried tangerine peel in the cellophane bags found in Chinese markets. Variations on

Habanero-Peach Preserves

While habaneros are fiery hot, this preserve has only a little heat – but shows off the chillies' ethereal tropical fruitiness to good advantage. If you crave more heat, just increase the number of habaneros (but be careful, they are seriously hot; wearing rubber gloves while chopping is a very sensible precaution as well).

Makes about 6 half-pint jars
6 cups (1 kg) peaches, peeled, stoned and chopped
2 habanero chillies, seeded and minced
3 cups (600 g) granulated sugar
1.5 tbsp fresh lemon juice
7 tbsp powered or liquid pectin (not instant)

Place the first four ingredients in a non-reactive pot. Cover with clingfilm, and refrigerate for at least two hours. Bring pot just to a simmer, then cool. Cover with clingfilm, and refrigerate overnight. Stir in pectin and boil for one minute, skimming and gently stirring. A little butter can be added to help minimize foaming. Pack into jelly jars, seal and process in a hot water bath for ten minutes.

douchi appear in the kitchens of Japan, Kampuchea (the former Cambodia), Korea, the Philippines and Vietnam.

Meats

Stocks are made by slowly simmering roasted bones – especially those of calves, which contain more collagen than the bones of adult animals – and *mirepoix*, an aromatic mixture of carrots, celery

Orange Marmalade (1839)

Grate fine the yellow peel from some ripe deep colored oranges, cut up all that are decorticated, saving the juice and removing the seeds and cores; mix with the pulp the grated peel, add an equal weight of powdered loaf sugar and a very little water, simmer the whole together till it becomes thick and quite transparent. When cold put up in small glass jars, and cover them with brandy papers.[16]

and onions. They are the foundation of classic French cookery. These protein-rich liquids could easily become a breeding place for bacteria if not kept safely out of the danger zone (5°–57.2°C /41°–135°F). When the stock is reduced to a firm gelatine, it becomes *glace de viand* that can last for months in a refrigerator. *Glace de volaille* and *glace de poisson* are the same, but made with chicken or fish, respectively.

In the late eighteenth and early nineteenth centuries, people like Nicolas Appert, Gail Borden and Alexis Soyer tried to develop similar concentrated or reduced beef extracts that could be stored indefinitely. Similar experiments with 'portable soups' had been carried out as early as 1690. These were old ideas that had been tried with varying degrees of success. Ghenghis Khan's Mongolian armies carried bags of *borts* – beef dried so hard that it could be powdered – in the thirteenth century ready to be reconstituted as needed.

Today we have many variations on the theme of stock (or soup) substitutes. Bouillon cubes, a mixture of dehydrated stock, salt, and hydrolysed vegetable protein, have been languishing in our pantries for over a century. We hope not the *original* supply, sold in 1908 (although, if stored properly, they might still be

Moroccan Preserved Lemons

This is one of the rare citrus recipes for which the white pith is not discarded. The pickling renders it succulent, with none of the bitterness we are always warned to avoid. It is almost impossible to imagine Moroccan cooking without little strips of these salty, velvety, tangy and fragrant lemon peels. Usually, only the rinds are used, but the pulp is loaded with flavour as well. They are always rinsed before use, to rid them of excess salt and any harmless white mould that might have formed on them.

Makes 1 quart (1 litre)
5 or 6 lemons, quartered lengthwise, lone end still attached
6 oz (170 g) salt
2 bay leaves
4 whole cloves
1 tsp coriander seeds
1 tsp black peppercorns

Squeeze the lemons into a bowl, reserving the juice. Place two tablespoons of salt into the bottom of the glass-topped jar (don't use a jar with a metal lid – salt and lemon juice will corrode it). Press a layer of lemons in the jar. Pour in more salt and part of the spices. Repeat until the jar is fully packed, and you have used all of the salt and spices. Seal the lid and allow to pickle in the refrigerator for four to six weeks. Preserved lemons are generally rinsed before using, and most Moroccan cooks discard the pulp and any seeds. They will last – if you don't use them all up first – for about six months. You can also add more lemons to the bottom of the pickling jar as space becomes available.

Fermented hot and sour mustard. Made in Thailand, for the Chinese market, of mustard greens with chillies, lime juice, soy sauce and sugar. Note that the illustration is not of the product, but the foods it is intended to accompany.

edible). Stocks of various kinds are now available canned, either in traditional tins or in plastic-lined paper containers. *Glace de viand* can even be found in little shelf-stable plastic cups that need no refrigeration. Liquid, or semi-liquid, versions of these meat extracts include Bonox and Panopepton (1918 and 1920s, respectively), and Bovril (1889) – originally called 'Johnson's Fluid Beef'. Today, these products contain less than 50 per cent meat – the remainder being made up of salt and yeast extracts. The company Maggi has produced a similar essence – without meat – based entirely on hydrolysed vegetable protein and salt since 1886. Marmite and Vegemite are other vegetarian umami-rich pastes made from spent brewer's yeasts.

Snack foods take up a lot of pantry space in our homes, and we don't begrudge them a bit of it. Think about what we love best about snack foods: they tend to be sweet and salty, they are often high in fat, they have concentrated flavours and many of them are dry enough to be crunchy. These are qualities often found in preserved foods. What is a crisp (a potato chip in the U.S.), if not a dehydrated vegetable, saturated with fat and salt? What is a Slim Jim, if not a commercially produced and cellophane-wrapped strip of *charqui*?

In recent years, food companies have tried to cash in on the popularity of dried fruits. They are handy, tasty and are perceived as being more 'natural' than other snack foods. 'Dried plums' are what used to be called, simply, 'prunes'. The old name has a senior-citizen whiff about it that marketers believe would not make the fruits appealing to shoppers wishing to remain forever young. Consequently, they were rechristened, and individually wrapped, as if they were just a healthier kind of sweet.

Squid – dried, shredded and heavily seasoned – is a popular snack food all around the Pacific basin. From Southeast Asia to Hong Kong, the Philippines, Japan and Hawaii, people munch on

Wasabi peas: freeze-dried, coated with a paste of rice starch, dehydrated horseradish (real wasabi is expensive), salt and green food colouring, then vacuum-packed in a can. An international and quintessentially modern preserved snack food.

Bovril poster, 1905.

them from plastic-sealed bags, or pair the chewy salty shreds with whatever form of alcohol is handy. In the West, free peanuts sit on the bar to stimulate thirst, just as tapas do in Spain, or olives in France. For the same reason, owners of cinemas exploit the thirst-provoking qualities of well-salted popcorn to encourage the sale of more lucrative soft drinks.

Less familiar to Non-Asians, *kaipen* is a crunchy snack made from freshwater algae. It is mixed with vegetables, such as garlic, spring onions or tomatoes, and seasoned with gingery galangal and sesame seeds. It is pressed into papery sheets that resemble the nori used to make sushi rolls. Crisply fried, it is the perfect food to munch on while drinking a cold one (or two). When the conquistadors entered the island that is now Mexico City for the first time, at the beginning of the sixteenth century, they saw similar foods being made from algae that grew in the lake.

Afterword

T he evolution of food preservation is geared, today, to reproducing, as closely as possible, the flavours and textures of the original foodstuffs. Older methods always altered their organoleptic properties – those which we perceive through our combined senses – often in ways that made them into new and different foods. Too many of us, I suspect, have forgotten that those differences are not necessarily faults, and that preserved foods should be judged on their own merits and not on whether they taste 'fresh'.

Most of the preserved foods discussed in this book do not even attempt to resemble their original foodstuffs. They are the quirky, often intensely flavoured foods and condiments produced by salting, drying and especially fermenting. They are foods that define moments in our collective past, or recreate the taste of exotic places. We treasure them because they are not like the bland mass-productions of the latest technologies.

All too easily, however, our favourite flavours can disappear, doomed to exist only as regret-filled nostalgia. We will conclude with an account of one such food we may never taste again.

Leiderkrantz was an early example of what we might call an 'artisanal cheese'. Soft-ripened and aromatic, with a firm crust, it was nothing like modern mass-produced processed cheeses. It was invented in response to a contest sponsored by a New York

City delicatessen owner, Adolphe Tode, who wanted to replace imported Bismarck Schlosskäse with a lower-priced domestic imitation. It was named for a German singing society in New York, and its popularity grew quickly. Eventually, its tiny dairy barn factory was replaced by larger quarters. At first, sterile conditions at the modern plant prevented the cheese from ripening or developing its characteristic bloom of mould. Legend has it that the original boards from the old plant were nailed up inside the sterile facility, and as much of the cheese as could be found on store shelves was smeared on the boards to recreate the proper biological environment for the cheese. Whatever actually occurred, they were able to restart the cultures and this wonderful cheese was saved.

For a while.

Borden's bought the rights to the cheese, adding their logo to the little yellow and white boxes. However, the stinky cheese market was too small for the corporate giant. They discontinued production in the early 1980s – ironically, just as Americans were beginning to develop a taste for something more sophisticated than bland, industrially produced 'cheesefood'. Borden's sold the rights, and the all-essential cultures, to a firm in Australia. Rumours circulate, every few years, that production of Leiderkrantz will begin again, but those of us who hold fond memories of this wonderfully smelly cheese have been disappointed every time.

Timeline

7000 BCE

Surplus grain from agriculture means that granaries and breweries start to become feasible and practical; in Latin America nixtamalization of maize is discovered, increasing that grain's nutritional properties; the Chinese start to cultivate rice shortly thereafter

5500 BCE

Wine begins to be made in what is now a mountainous region of Iran

5000 BCE (or possibly even earlier)

The first cheeses are produced

4500 BCE

Salt and alkaline minerals are used to remove the bitterness from olives and oil is pressed from them

2500 BCE

The Mesopotamians realize that vinegar can be used to preserve vegetables as pickles

2000 BCE

Central Americans learn to ferment, dry and pulverize the pods of Theobroma cacao, making xocoatl, the first chocolate drink

1600 BCE

Mesopotamians salt meats to preserve them

1500 BCE

The Chinese salt down pork bellies, not just to preserve them but because they prefer their flavour over that of fresh pork

600 BCE

Asians begin to make dozens of new fermented seasoning ingredients, jiang, first from meats and fish, and later from soy and wheat

500 BCE

The juice of wild grasses of the Saccharum genus – which grow all around the Asian subcontinent – is evaporated to form crystals of sugar in northern India. A thousand years later, it has reached the Middle East and, after another 1,000 years, the New World provides a perfect place for growing sugar cane

400 CE

The Romans make sauces spiked with mustard. Like most Roman condiments, they contain a bit of liquamen

700

Koreans salt cabbage and other vegetables into their national food, kimchi (though it is nearly a millennium before they have any chillies to throw into the pots)

1000

The Chinese learn to substitute tofu – from soya beans – for meat. Salt cod begins to serve the same purpose in northern Europe. Curiously, both vegetarian options were based on religion, one Buddhist, the other Christian

1500

A craze for coffee spreads from Ethiopia and Yemen to the capitals of Europe. This is roughly the time that tea becomes popular, as well as hot chocolate. Europe discovers its love for all of its hot beverages at once, and beer loses its monopoly as the only safe way to drink water

1900

Improved technologies for canning and freezing make seasonal foods almost a thing of the past

1950

Improved transportation and international trade on a formerly unimaginable scale make fresh seasonal foods a thing of the past. Ironically modern science also makes more varieties of preserved food available than at any time in history

1958

First commercial use of radiation to preserve food

1970

Pascalization – the preservation of food using only ultra-high pressure – is first used commercially. The process had been used experimentally at the end of the nineteenth century, but never made it to market

References

Introduction

1 Mark Bittman, 'Not All Industrial Food Is Evil', *New York Times*, 17 August 2013, http://opinionator.blogs.nytimes.com.
2 Elatia Harris, 'Food and Power: An Interview with Rachel Laudan', www.3quarksdaily.com, accessed 7 October 2015.

1 Perils

1 Nadia Arumugam, 'Why American Eggs Would Be Illegal in a British Supermarket, And Vice Versa', *Forbes*, 25 October 2012, www.forbes.com.
2 Ibid.
3 Anonymous, *A Queens Delight; Or, The Art of Preserving, Conserving and Candying* (London, 1671), available at www.gutenberg.org.
4 Ibid.

2 Ancient Preserving Methods

1 Gary Allen, *Sausage: A Global History* (London, 2015).
2 Mark Kurlansky, *Salt: A World History* (New York, 2002), p. 137.
3 *Cassell's Dictionary of Cookery* (*c.* 1870), quoted in Janet Clarkson, 'Butter and Honey', www.theoldfoodie.com.
4 Hannah Woolley, *The Cook's Guide; Or, Rare Receipts for Cookery* (1664), quoted in Janet Clarkson, 'Half a Bucke', www.theoldfoodie.com.
5 Ibid.

3 Modern Preserving Methods

1 Genevieve Wanucha, 'Two Happy Clams', MIT *news magazine* (24 February 2009), www.technologyreview.com.

2 Gary Allen, 'Armour', in *Encyclopedia of Food and Drink in America*, 2nd edn (Oxford and New York, 2012).

3 Marc Santora, 'Tuberculosis Cases Prompt Warning on Raw-milk Cheese', *New York Times*, 16 March 2005, www.nytimes.com.

4 Daniel J. Boorstin, *The Americans: The Democratic Experience* (New York, 1973), p. 313.

5 Ibid.

4 Major Ingredients

1 *The Widowes Treasure . . .* (1588), quoted at www.theoldfoodie.com.

2 Mrs N.K.M. Lee and Eliza Lee, *The Cook's Own Book, and Housekeeper's Register* (1832), quoted at www.theoldfoodie.com.

3 Gary Allen, *Sausage: A Global History* (London, 2015), p. 71.

4 Guillaume Tirel, *Le Viandier de Taillevent*, trans. James Prescott (Eugene, OR, 1989), pp. 27–8, www.telusplanet.net.

5 James Robinson, *The Whole Art of Curing, Pickling, and Smoking Meat and Fish* (London, 1847), p. 58, available at https://archive.org.

6 Hannah Glasse, *The Art of Cookery Made Plain and Easy; Which Far Exceeds Any Thing of the Kind Yet Published* (London, 1774), online at https://google.com/books, pp. 366–7.

7 Mrs Isabella Beeton, *The Book of Household Management* (London, 1861), available at www.gutenberg.org.

8 Janet Clarkson, 'Preserved Beef, Otherwayes', 2 September 2009, www.theoldfoodie.com.

9 William Andrus Alcott, *The Young House-keeper: or, Thoughts on Food and Cookery* (Boston, 1846), p. 204, online at http://digital.lib.msu.edu.

10 Mark Kurlansky, *Cod: A Biography of the Fish that Changed the World* (New York, 1997), p. 21.

11 Eileen Power, trans., *The Goodman of Paris: A Treatise on Moral and Domestic Economy by a Citizen of Paris, c. 1393* (Rochester, NY, 2006), p. 179.

12 Mark Kurlansky, *Salt: A World History* (New York, 2002), p. 137.
13 Ibid.
14 William Butler Yeats, 'The Meditation of the Old Fisherman' [1886] www.theotherpages.org.
15 Glasse, *The Art of Cookery Made Plain and Easy*, pp. 229–30.
16 Te-Ping Chen. 'Off the Menu: Hong Kong Government Bans Shark's Fin', *Wall Street Journal, ChinaRealtimeReport*, 16 September 2013, http://blogs.wsj.com.
17 Eliza Leslie, *Directions for Cookery, in its Various Branches* (Philadelphia, PA, 1840), available at www.gutenberg.org, pp. 67.
18 Ibid., pp. 30–31.
19 Elisabeth Townsend, *Lobster: A Global History* (London, 2011), p. 18.
20 Bruce Kraig and Patty Carol, *Man Bites Dog: Hot Dog Culture in America* (Lanham, MD, and Plymouth, 2012), p. 13.
21 Robert May, *The Accomplisht Cook; or The Art and Mystery of Cookery* (London, 1685), available at www.gutenberg.org.
22 Maria Eliza Rundell, *Domestic Economy, and Cookery, for Rich and Poor; Containing an Account of the Best English, Scotch, French, Oriental, and other Foreign Dishes; Preparations of Broths and Milks for Consumption; Receipts for Sea-faring Men. Travellers, and Children's Food. Together with Estimates and Comparisons of Dinners and Dishes. The Whole Composed with the Utmost Attention to Health, Economy, and Elegance. By a Lady* (London, 1827), p. 618.
23 John Bostock and Henry Thomas Riley, trans., *The Natural History of Pliny* (London, 1856–93), vol. III, p. 84, www.perseus.tufts.edu.
24 Ibid.
25 Janet Clarkson, 'The Invention of "American Cheese"', 10 December 2007, www.theoldfoodie.com.
26 Nadia Arumugam, 'Why American Eggs Would Be Illegal in a British Supermarket, And Vice Versa', *Forbes*, 25 October 2012, www.forbes.com.
27 *Eggs: Facts and Fancies About Them* (1890), quoted at www.theoldfoodie.com.
28 Arumagan, 'Why American Eggs'.
29 *Henley's Twentieth Century Book of Recipes, Formulas, and Processes* (1916), quoted in *The Old Foodie*, www.theoldfoodie.com.

30 Ibid.
31 'Dole Food Company, Inc. History', *International Directory of Company Histories*, LXVIII (Farmington Hills, MI, 2005), www.fundinguniverse.com.
32 Society of Gentlemen, *The Universal Receipt Book* (New York, 1814), quoted in Sally Smith Booth, *Hung, Strung, and Potted: A History of Eating Habits in Colonial America* (New York, 1971), p. 164.
33 Mrs Meer Hassan Ali, *Observations on the Mussulmauns of India: Descriptive of Their Manners, Customs, Habits and Religious Opinions Made During a Twelve Years' Residence in Their Immediate Society*, 2nd edn (1917), available at www.gutenberg.org.
34 Ibid.
35 Stacey Shackford, 'Biomolecular Archaeologist Uncorks World's Oldest Known Grape Wine', *Ezra Update*, May 2012, http://ezramagazine.cornell.edu.
36 James H. Collins, *The Story of Canned Foods*, quoted in Sue Shephard, *Pickled, Potted, and Canned: How the Art and Science of Food Preserving Changed the World* (New York, 2006), p. 247.
37 Quoted in Hilary Spurling, *Elinor Fettiplace's Receipt Book: Elizabethan Country House Cooking* (New York, 1987), p. 173.
38 Eliza Smith, *The Compleat Housewife; Or, Accomplish'd Gentlewoman's Companion*, 9th edn (London 1739), available at https://google.com/books, p. 94.
39 Ibid.
40 Daniel Patterson, 'Hocus Pocus and a Beaker of Truffles', *New York Times*, 16 May 2007, www.nytimes.com.

5 Geography

1 Yu-Xiao Zhu et al., 'Geography and Similarity of Regional Cuisines in China', http://arxiv.org/abs/1307.3185, accessed 15 October 2015.
2 Michaeleen Doucleff, 'Ancient Wine Bar? Giant Jugs Of Vino Unearthed In 3,700-year-old Cellar', *The Salt: What's on Your Plate*, www.npr.org.
3 Karen Hess, *The Carolina Kitchen: The African Connection* (Columbia, SC, 1992), pp. 3–4.

4 Cynthia Bertelsen, 'Flavor Principles Out of Africa: A Fish Tale', *Gerkins & Tomatoes*, 4 June 2009, http://gherkinstomatoes.com.

5 Wolfgang Fassbender, 'Graen in der Dose', *Nachgewürzt*, 22 August 2011, http://nachgewuerzt.blog.nzz.ch.

6 Janet Clarkson, 'American Food in London, 1939', 14 August 2013, www.theoldfoodie.com.

7 Jonathan Rees, 'The Huge Chill: Why Are American Refrigerators So Big?', *Atlantic Mobile*, 4 October 2013, http://m.theatlantic. com.

8 Marvin Harris, *Cows, Pigs, Wars and Witches: The Riddles of Culture* (New York, 1974), pp. 28-50.

9 *Domestic Economy, and Cookery, for Rich and Poor, by a Lady* (London, 1827), online at http://books.google.com/books, p. 618.

10 Priscilla Homespun, *The Universal Receipt Book: Being a Compendious Repository of Practical Information in Cookery, Preserving, Pickling, Distilling, and all the Branches of Domestic Economy. To Which is Added, Some Advice to Farmers* (Philadelphia, PA, 1818), available at https://google.com/books, p. 169.

11 Leslie, *Directions for Cookery*.

12 John Evelyn, *Acetaria: A Discourse of Sallets* (London, 1699), online at https://books.google.com/books, p. 806.

6 Beyond the Main Course

1 Richard Ligon, *A True and Exact History of the Island of Barbados* (London, 1657), http://books.google.com/books, p. 75, accessed 15 October 2015.

2 John Evelyn, *Acetaria: A Discourse of Sallets* (London, 1699), https://google.com/books, p. 113.

3 Christopher Grocock and Sally Grainger, *Apicius: A Critical Edition with an Introduction and an English Translation of the Latin Recipe Text Apicius* (Devon, 2006), p. 139.

4 Jai Kharbanda and Anda Lincoln, 'Chicha', in *The Oxford Companion to Beer*, ed. Garrett Oliver (New York, 2011), pp. 242–3.

5 Albert Idell, trans., *The Bernal Díaz Chronicles: The True Story of the Conquest of Mexico* (New York, 1956), p. 150.

6   'Letters and Papers on Agriculture, Planting, &c: Selected
    from the Correspondence of the Society Instituted at Bath, for
    the Encouragement of Agriculture, Arts, Manufactures and
    Commerce, Within the Counties of Somerset, Wilts, Gloucester,
    and Dorset, and the City and County of Bristol, 1790', quoted in
    Janet Clarkson, 'Butter and Honey', www.theoldfoodie.com.
7   Eliza Leslie, *Directions for Cookery, in its Various Branches*
    (Philadelphia, PA, 1840), www.gutenberg.org, p. 173.
8   'How We Make Original Red Sauce', www.tabasco.com.
9   Hannah Glasse, *The Art of Cookery Made Plain and Easy; Which
    Far Exceeds Any Thing of the Kind Yet Published* (London, 1774),
    pp. 308–9.
10 Mary Randolph, *The Virginia Housewife or Methodical Cook*
    (Philadelphia, PA, 1860), facsimile edition (New York, 1993), p. 162.
11 C. Martinelli, trans., *An Anonymous Andalusian Cookbook from the
    13th Century*, http://italophiles.com/andalusian_cookbook.pdf.
12 Ibid.
13 Mrs Meer Hassan Ali, *Observations on the Mussulmauns of India:
    Descriptive of Their Manners, Customs, Habits and Religious Opinions
    Made During a Twelve Years' Residence in Their Immediate Society*,
    2nd edn (1917), www.gutenberg.org, p. 200, accessed 16 October
    2015.
14 Jennifer Burns Levin, 'Mixed Pickle: The Sweet and Sour Legacy
    of Dutch Trade', *NPR: The Salt*, 18 January 2014, online at www.
    npr.org.
15 Thomas G. Fessenden, *The New England Farmer*, vol. 1 (Boston,
    MA, 1823), https://books.google.com/books, p. 330, accessed
    16 October 2015.
16 Lettice Bryan, *The Kentucky Housewife* (Cincinnati, OH, 1839),
    http:// books.google.com, p. 360.

Bibliography

Alcott, William Andrus, *The Young House-Keeper: or, Thoughts on Food and Cookery* (Boston, MA, 1846), http://digital.lib.msu.edu/projects/cookbooks

Ali, Mrs Meer Hassan, *Observations on the Mussulmauns of India: Descriptive of Their Manners, Customs, Habits and Religious Opinions Made During a Twelve Years' Residence in Their Immediate Society*, 2nd edn (1917), www.gutenberg.org

Allen, Ann H., *The Orphan's Friend and Housekeeper's Assistant Is Composed Upon Temperance Principles: With Instructions in the Art of Making Plain and Fancy Cakes, Puddings, Pastry Confectionery, Ice Creams, Jellies, Blanc Mange: Also for the Cooking of All the Various Meats and Vegetables: With a Variety of Useful Information and Receipts Never Before Published* (Boston, MA, 1845)

Allen, Gary, *The Herbalist in the Kitchen* (Urbana, IL, 2007)

—, 'Armour', in *Encyclopedia of Food and Drink in America*, ed. Andrew F. Smith, 2nd edn (Oxford and New York, 2012)

—, *Sausage: A Global History* (London, 2015)

Arumugam, Nadia, 'Why American Eggs Would Be Illegal in a British Supermarket, And Vice Versa', *Forbes* (25 October 2012), www.forbes.com

Bad Bug Book, Foodborne Pathogenic Microorganisms and Natural Toxins, 2nd edn (Washington, DC, 2012), online at www.fda.gov

Beeton, Mrs Isabella, *The Book of Household Management* (London, 1861), www.gutenberg.org

Bentley, Amy, *Eating for Victory: Food Rationing and the Politics of Domesticity* (Urbana and Chicago, IL, 1998)

Bertelsen, Cynthia, 'Flavor Principles Out of Africa: A Fish Tale', 4 June 2009, online at http://gherkinstomatoes.com

Bittman, Mark, 'Not All Industrial Food Is Evil', *New York Times*, 17 August 2013, http://opinionator.blogs.nytimes.com

Boorstin, Daniel J., *The Americans: The Democratic Experience* (New York, 1973)

Booth, Sally Smith, *Hung, Strung, and Potted: A History of Eating Habits in Colonial America* (New York, 1971)

Bostock, John, and Henry Thomas Riley, trans., *The Natural History of Pliny* (London, 1856–93), online at www.perseus.tufts.edu

Bottéro, Jean, *The Oldest Cuisine in the World: Cooking in Mesopotamia* (Chicago, IL, and London, 2004)

Bryan, Lettice, *The Kentucky Housewife* (Cincinnati, OH, 1839), http://books.google.com

Chen, Te-Ping, 'Off the Menu: Hong Kong Government Bans Shark's Fin', *Wall Street Journal*, *ChinaRealtimeReport*, 16 September 2013, http://blogs.wsj.com

Clarkson, Janet, 'American Food in London, 1939', 14 August 2013, www.theoldfoodie.com

—, 'The Curious Secret of Making Artificial Olives', 1 November 2013, www.theoldfoodie.com

—, 'Half a Bucke', 17 July 2006, www.theoldfoodie.com

—, 'Preserved Beef, Otherwayes', 2 September 2009, www.theoldfoodie.com

—, 'Preserving Eggs, Otherwayes', 6 April 2007, www.theoldfoodie.com

Culinary Institute of America, *Olive Oil: A Guide for Culinary Professionals* (Hyde Park, NY, n.d.)

Danhi, Robert, 'Authentic Asian', *Prepared Foods*, September 2013, www.preparedfoods.com

'Dole Food Company, Inc. History', *International Directory of Company Histories*, LXVI (Farmington Hills, MI, 2005), www.fundinguniverse.com

Domestic Economy, and Cookery, for Rich and Poor, by a Lady (London, 1827), https://books.google.com/books, accessed 15 October 2015

Doucleff, Michaeleen, 'Ancient Wine Bar? Giant Jugs of Vino Unearthed in 3,700-year-old Cellar', *The Salt: What's on Your Plate*, www.npr.org

Evelyn, John, *Acetaria: A Discourse of Sallets* (London, 1699)

Fassbender, Wolfgang, 'Graen in der Dose', *Nachgewürzt* (22 August 2011), http://nachgewuerzt.blog.nzz.ch

Fessenden, Thomas G., *The New England Farmer*, vol. 1 (Boston, 1823)

'Food Irradiation', U.S. Environmental Protection Agency, www.epa.gov

Galloway, J. H., 'Sugar', in *The Cambridge World History of Food*, ed. Kenneth Kiple and Kriemhild Conée Ornelas (Cambridge, 2000), downloadable at www.panelamonitor.org, accessed 7 October 2015

Glasse, Hannah, *The Art of Cookery Made Plain and Easy; Which Far Exceeds Any Thing of the Kind Yet Published* (London, 1774)

Gray, Melissa, 'Listeria Outbreak Linked to Cheese; 1 dead, 4 sickened', www.cnn.com

Grocock, Christopher, and Sally Grainger, *Apicius: A Critical Edition with an Introduction and an English Translation of the Latin Recipe Text Apicius* (Devon, 2006)

Harris, Elatia, 'Food and Power: An Interview with Rachel Laudan', www.3quarksdaily.com

Harris, Marvin, *Cows, Pigs, Wars and Witches: The Riddles of Culture* (New York, 1974)

Heiss, Mary Lou, and Robert J. Heiss, *The Story of Tea: A Cultural History and Drinking Guide* (Berkeley, CA, and Toronto, 2007)

Hess, Karen, *The Carolina Kitchen: The African Connection* (Columbia, SC, 1992)

Homespun, Priscilla, *The Universal Receipt Book: Being a Compendious Repository of Practical Information in Cookery, Preserving, Pickling, Distilling, and all the Branches of Domestic Economy. To Which is Added, Some Advice to Farmers* (Philadelphia, PA, 1818)

Idell, Albert, trans., *The Bernal Díaz Chronicles: The True Story of the Conquest of Mexico* (New York, 1956)

International Cocoa Organization, 'How Does the Fermentation Process Work on the Cocoa Bean and How Long does it Take?', 28 August 1998, www.icco.org

Katz, Sandor Ellis, *The Art of Fermentation* (White River Junction, VT, 2012)

Kelly, Laura, 'Making Kimchi', *The Silk Road Gourmet*, 9 January 2012, www.silkroadgourmet.com

Kim, Evelyn, 'The Amazing Multimillion-year History of Processed Food', *Scientific American* (September 2013), pp. 50–55

Kraig, Bruce, and Patty Carroll, *Man Bites Dog* (Lanham, MD, and Plymouth, 2012)

Kurlansky, Mark, *Cod: A Biography of the Fish that Changed the World* (New York, 1997)

—, *Salt: A World History* (New York, 2002)

Laszlo, Pierre, *Salt: Grain of Life*, trans. Mary Beth Mader (New York, 2001)

Laughton, James W., *The General Receipt Book: Containing an Extensive Collection of Valuable Receipts, Connected with Domestic Economy* (1853), online at https://archive.org

Leroy, Frédéric, et al., 'Meat Fermentation at the Crossroads of Innovation and Tradition: A Historical Outlook', www.academia.edu

Leslie, Eliza, *Directions for Cookery, in its Various Branches: Forty-ninth Edition, Thoroughly Revised with Additions* (Philadelphia, PA, 1853)

Levin, Jennifer Burns, 'Mixed Pickle: The Sweet and Sour Legacy of Dutch Trade', *NPR: The Salt*, online at www.npr.org

Ligon, Richard, *A True & Exact History of the Island of Barbados* (London, 1657), http://davidchansmith.net/the-richard-ligon-project

Lorenzi, Rossella, '3,000-year-old Butter Discovered in Ireland', www.nbcnews.com

McGee, Harold, 'A Festive Ferment', *Nature*, DIV/372–4, www.nature.com

Mamta's Kitchen, 'Lemon Pickle 1, in Oil', www.mamtaskitchen.com

Martinelli, C., trans., *An Anonymous Andalusian Cookbook from the 13th Century*, http://italophiles.com

May, Robert, *The Accomplisht Cook, or the Art & Mystery of Cookery* (London, 1685), www.gutenberg.org

Oliver, Garrett, ed., *The Oxford Companion to Beer* (New York, 2011)

Patterson, Daniel, 'Hocus Pocus and a Beaker of Truffles', *New York Times* (16 May 2007), www.nytimes.com

Pendergrast, Mark, *Uncommon Grounds: The History of Coffee and How It Transformed Our World* (New York, 1999)

Peñarrieta, J. Mauricio, et al., 'Chuño and Tunta: The Traditional Andean Sun-dried Potatoes', www.researchgate.net

Poulson, Bo, *Dutch Herring: An Environmental History, c. 1600–1860* (Amsterdam, 2008)

Power, Eileen, trans., *The Goodman of Paris: A Treatise on Moral and Domestic Economy by a Citizen of Paris, c. 1393* (Rochester, NY, 2006)

Praderio, Caroline, 'Nitrites & Nitrates: Are They Harmful or Actually Healthful?' *Prevention*, January 2015, www.prevention.com

A Queens Delight; Or, The Art of Preserving, Conserving and Candying (London, 1671), www.gutenberg.org

Randolph, Mary, *The Virginia Housewife or Methodical Cook* (Philadelphia, PA, 1860); Dover facsimile edn (New York, 1993)

Rao, S. V. Suryanarayana, A. P. Valsan and M. Rajemjranathan Nayar, 'Studies on the Preservation of Fish by Pickling', *Indian Journal of Fisheries*, pp. 326–40, http://eprints.cmfri.org.in/1842/1/Article_10.pdf

Rees, Jonathan, 'The Huge Chill: Why Are American Refrigerators So Big?', *Atlantic*, 4 October 2013, online at www.theatlantic.com

Robinson, James, *The Whole Art of Curing, Pickling, and Smoking Meat and Fish* (London, 1847), https://archive.org

Rundell, Maria Eliza, *Domestic Economy, and Cookery, for Rich and Poor; Containing an Account of the Best English, Scotch, French, Oriental, and other Foreign Dishes; Preparations of Broths and Milks for Consumption; Receipts for Sea-Faring Men. Travellers, and Children's Food. Together with Estimates and Comparisons of Dinners and Dishes. The Whole Composed with the Utmost Attention to Health, Economy, and Elegance. By a Lady* (London, 1827)

Santora, Marc, 'Tuberculosis Cases Prompt Warning on Raw-milk Cheese', *New York Times* (16 March 2005), www.nytimes.com

Shackford, Stacey, 'Biomolecular Archaeologist Uncorks World's Oldest Known Grape Wine', *Ezra Update*, May 2012, http://ezramagazine.cornell.edu

Shephard, Sue, *Pickled, Potted, and Canned: How the Art and Science of Food Preserving Changed the World* (New York, 2006)

Smith, Andrew F., *Souper Tomatoes* (New Brunswick, NJ, 2000)

Smith, Eliza, *The Compleat Housewife; Or, Accomplish'd Gentlewoman's Companion*, 9th edn (London, 1739)

Spurling, Hilary, *Elinor Fettiplace's Receipt Book: Elizabethan Country House Cooking* (New York, 1987)

Tabasco, 'How We Make Original Red Sauce', www.tabasco.com

Tirel, Guillaume, *Le Viandier de Taillevent*, trans. James Prescott
(Eugene, OR, 1989), www.telusplanet.net

Townsend, Elisabeth, *Lobster: A Global History* (London, 2011)

Trafton, Anne, 'Canned, Good', *MIT News*, 12 January 2011,
http://newsoffice.mit.edu

USDA, 'Food Safety and Inspection Service', www.fsis.usda.gov

Walsh, John Henry, *The English Cookery Book: Uniting a Good Style
with Economy, and Adapted to All Persons in Every Clime* (1859).
Quoted in www.theoldfoodie.com

Wanucha, Genevieve, 'Two Happy Clams', *MIT News Magazine*
(24 February 2009), www.technologyreview.com

*The Widowes Treasure Plentifully Furnished with Sundry Precious
and Aprooued Secretes in Phisicke and Chirurgery for the Health
and Pleasure of Mankinde: Hereunto are Adioyned, Sundry Pretie
Practises and Conclusions of Cookerie; with Many Profitable and
Holesome Medicines for Sundrie Diseases in Cattell* (1588). Quoted
in www.theoldfoodie.com

Weinstein, Bruce, and Mark Scarborough, *An Obsession with Ham the
Hindquarter* (New York, 2010)

Winters, Ruth, *A Consumer's Dictionary of Food Additives*, 4th edn
(New York, 1994)

Yeasts and Moulds Associated with Premature Food Spoilage, https://
fscimage.fishersci.com/images/D10079~.pdf, accessed
7 October 2015

Zhu, Yu-Xiao, et al., 'Geography and Similarity of Regional Cuisines in
China', http://arxiv.org/abs/1307.3185, accessed 7 October 2015

Other Resources

Museum and Exhibits

Spreewald Pickle Museum
Hotelantage Starick
Bauerenhaus- und Gurkenmuseum
An der Dolzke 6
03222 Lehde
Germany

Websites

Cookbook of Unknown Ladies, The
http://lostcookbook.wordpress.com/

Old Foodie, The
www.theoldfoodie.com

Well Preserved
http://wellpreserved.ca

Blogs and Other Social Media

Archaeological and Historical Foods (and a little archaeobotany!)
www.facebook.com/groups/451905478184482

The Cult of Pre-Pasteurian Preservation and Food Preparation
www.facebook.com/groups/111065265611664

Food in Jars
http://foodinjars.com

The Salt Cured Pig
www.facebook.com/groups/125499327503217

Acknowledgements

We live in an age where people are naturally suspicious of anything that might be secretly financed promotions of products mentioned in the media. I have not received – nor do I *expect* to receive – any incentives for including the names or images of any products in this book. No cash, no free goods, no all-expenses-paid trips to fabulous destinations. Alas!

I have, however, received other forms of support while researching this book, and for that I am grateful.

I am especially indebted to certain food historians. Janet Clarkson (and her blog, The Old Foodie) are both endlessly erudite and informative – not to mention entertaining. Likewise, Ken Albala is always available with appetizing bits of arcana, which includes his Facebook group, The Cult of Pre-Pasteurian Preservation and Food Preparation. Cynthia Bertelsen and *her* blog, Gherkins & Tomatoes, have provided insights and photographs I would not have found elsewhere – and her friend Marlon Kamagi, for his insider's account of fish preservation in Indonesia. A manuscript in London's Westminster City Archives – *The Cookbook of Unknown Ladies* – has provided several leads (and unusual recipes).

I could not ask for better role models, fact-checkers, fakelore debunkers and providers of moral support than Anne Mendelson and Andy Smith. Michael Leaman, Martha Jay and the entire production team at Reaktion Books, have provided wise counsel and general good advice throughout this and other projects.

As always, I have relied heavily on past colleagues at The Culinary Institute of America, especially chefs Robert Danhi and Bob Delgrosso – and, of course, the librarians at the CIA's Conrad Hilton Library, the

State University of New York at New Paltz's Sojourner Truth Library, and the New York Public Library.

Aaron Rester and Kate Krajci have aided and abetted my penchant for unusual foods in Chicago, as have Deborah Begley and Tamara Watson in Ithaca, New York. It's a source of constant amazement that they have willingly borne my repeated impositions (consequently, they can expect to be rewarded with more of the same in the future).

Finally, there's one person who has endured a life of unfamiliar and often odoriferous foods, accompanied by long periods of silence broken only by my endless key taps and occasional mild (sometimes not so mild) oaths. Her patient martyrdom, in regard to these and innumerable other offences, is among the reasons I refer to my wife as the 'sainted Karen Philipp'.

Photo Acknowledgements

The author and the publishers wish to express their thanks to the below sources of illustrative material and/or permission to reproduce it.

Gary Allen: pp. 14, 16, 32, 37, 39, 65, 83 top, 95, 98, 103, 114, 139 bottom left, 140, 156, 195, 200, 201, 202, 216, 217, 221, 226, 227; Cynthia Bertelson: pp. 29, 99, 100, 101; Delia du Plessis: p. 70; iStockphoto: pp. 139 (Handmade Pictures) bottom right, 143 (Etienne Voss); Library of Congress, Washington, DC: pp. 9, 10; Moonsun1981: p. 148; National Library and Archives of Quebec: p. 15; Karen Resta collection: p. 78; Samuell: p. 57; Schellack: p. 90; Shutterstock: pp. 6 (Kira Volkov), 79 (digitalreflections), 141 (Maya Kruchankova), 145 (Cesc Garcia), 151 (Sheila Fitzgerald), 155, 212 (Claudio Divizia); Stegen: pp. 74, 75, 76, 80, 83 bottom; Thinkstock: p. 97 (Polka Dot Images); Wellcome Library, London: p. 136.

Index

Page numbers in *italic* indicate illustrations;
page numbers in **bold** indicate recipes